THE JUDGMENT
OF GOD UPON
AMERICA

Dr. E. E. DeWitt

REL067030: Religion: Christian Theology – Apologetics.

ISBN: 978-1-7371005-4-6

All Scripture quotes are from the King James Bible except those verses compared and then the source is identified.

Address All Inquiries To:
THE OLD PATHS PUBLICATIONS, Inc.
142 Gold Flume Way
Cleveland, Georgia, U.S.A. 30528
Web: www.theoldpathspublications.com
E-mail: **TOP@theoldpathspublications.com**

1.0

DEDICATION

"Dedicated to the memory of Bro. John Carlson, long time pastor of Bethany Baptist Church of Galesburg, Il. Breaking with the teaching of the school he attended, Bro. Carlson always spoke from the King James Version, founded upon the preserved Traditional Text of God rather than the Critical Text of man. "That your faith should not stand in the wisdom of men, but in the power of God." Second Corinthians 2:5."

PREFACE

THE JUDGMENT OF GOD UPON AMERICA

This work was originally prepared for the 2020 Dean Burgon Society Bible Conference held just outside of Atlanta, Georgia. Unfortunately, covid 19 interfered. The live conference was replaced with an online version. I am not a "tech person." I am the type of person who will often return to my house before I try to drive off as I realize that I do not have my hand crank with me and will be unable to start my car without it.

When we switched from a "live" conference to an "online" version, I was left "offline" without the wherewithal to continue. I missed the conference. On the bright side, this was probably better for those who did attend. To be brutally honest, I am somewhat well below the expertise of the worst of the worst of the men who did speak.

I should note that there are no "worst" among these speakers; they are all first-rate orators and theologians. All are worthy of our attention and instruction. The only exception occurs when I am one of the speakers.

Still, I did consider my subject matter, if not myself, as worthy of consideration. Therefore, I have updated this message, greatly expanded it, and offer the information in this form!

TABLE OF CONTENTS

INTRODUCTION

RIGHTEOUSNESS EXALTETH A NATION BUT SIN IS A REPROACH TO ANY PEOPLE - Proverbs 14:34

With a title such as I have chosen for this work, one would expect me to begin with a section detailing the judgments of God upon our nation. I would consider that it would be a mistake to 3thus begin. Instead, I believe that it would be proper to heed the wise counsel of the Apostle Paul from First Corinthians 14:40, "Let all things be done decently and in order."

Under that distinctive I would believe that the proper beginning to such a study would be to invoke the Order of the Day of the Army of the Redeemed. My military background tells me to consider that which is the most important part of our duty to God, which is part of our daily walk whether in an "end-times" scenario or at every point of our Christian lives while we live unto the Lord in this present life. Second Timothy 2:15 would counsel us to rightly divide the Word of Truth. Even as we study the truth of a coming era, we must never lose sight of that which God has for us in that era in which we presently reside. Our first purpose as followers of the Lord is to seek to win others to His salvation. That is an *always* consideration. That is that which must be our purpose at all times.

With this in mind, I begin our study with a section describing our duty in calling others to salvation. Learning of God's time table for a future era is of little use to one who would find his soul lost in a Christless eternity. We need to equip our lives with the proclaiming of the essential truth that Jesus died in time so that others might live in eternity.

With this first established we may move on to consider the vows which our nation has made to the Lord of Eternity.

It is also wise to keep in mind that we are not a *Covenant People*

9

of God. This necessitates a need to establish just who is the people of that eternal Covenant. Still, while we might not be a covenant people of God, we are a people who have made certain vows to God. These vows do not make us a special people to God in the sense of covenant status. But, by the assuming of such political and personal vows, we have acknowledged that we have made a vow of fidelity to God. This is also foundational to the thesis of this study.

Keeping in mind the true identity of the Covenant People of God, is a view we have begun to disregard in recent years. This, in itself, is indicative of a great national sin which has called the judgment of God upon our nation. We have departed from the great truth of Genesis 12:3. While calling the people of Abraham to be a Covenant people unto Him, God gave the promise to the descendants of Abraham: "And I will bless them that bless thee, and curse him that curseth thee: and in thee shall all families of the earth be blessed."

To not honor, properly honor, the people who God has especially called from all the nations of the earth is to bring dishonor to God.

Further, a consideration of our own nation as a leading power in the world at this time, while realizing that we are not listed as a world-power, in those end-time prophecies will lead us to conclude that we must fall from our perch as a great power in the tribulation era. This is an inescapable consideration as we view prophecy.

When we couple this truth with the fact that our many national sins have invited the judgment of God. We should also take a look at some of those sins which give lie to our claim to keep the vows we have made to God. A listing, with a short description of those sins, must be included in our list.

What a great and glorious day the Lord has given us. Of course. any day that we are allowed to serve the Lord of All Glory is a great and glorious day, isn't it? So, I greet you in the Name that is above all names: The Messiah, Lord Jesus of Nazareth.

To be honest, calling Him "Jesus of Nazareth" is short-changing His Glory in our speech. It is true that He was of Nazareth in His humanity. But, in reality, in His eternal essence He IS, not "was." the very God of creation.

It is indeed glorious that we do serve a risen Savior Who is in the world today. The old song said it best. I won't attempt to sing that song; I am hard enough to listen to when I simply speak. To attempt so sing would not lull you to sleep; it would launch you from you seats so quickly that some might be injured.

We pray to Him and He does answer us in this world of time and physicality. His answer may be by bringing to mind a familiar verse of Scripture. That is just one more reason that we should work to memorize those precious words of inspired and preserved Scripture. He may answer by the actions we may witness upon this earth. One thing is certain; if we are attuned to His presence, we will hear His still, small voice from the cave of our existence.

John 3: 13 tells us,

> *"And no man hath ascended up to heaven, but he that came down from heaven. even the Son of man which is in heaven."*

He was on earth speaking with Nicodemus in ancient Jerusalem even as He was in Heaven. That verse speaks of the deity of Jesus.

Although, as God, He fills the Heavens and the created universe, Heaven is now His Special Place of residence. He is of the spiritual and eternal order of existence. We are from this earth of physicality and time. It is a miracle of grace and His glory that He interacts with us on this earth in this Dispensation of Time.

It is generally true that we will not hear His audible voice. Our residence within this time-centric and physical reality of the created universe will hinder this reality. I use the word "generally" because I do not limit the power of Almighty God. He can do what He wishes. I do recognize that we do have limitations within our physicality and should not expect such an answer. Still, God can override my theology at any point He might find a purpose to do so!

John 1:3 reminds of that Jesus is the creative force of the Triune Godhead.

> *"All things were made by him and without Him was not anything made that was made."*

We must remember that Jesus is not a created being. He is the Being Who created all. Also, First John 2:2 reminds us of Him.

> *"And he is the propitiation for our sins: and not for ours only, but also for the sins of the whole world."*

But it is evident that not all are saved. Why?

So, if it is true - and the Bible says that it is - that Jesus died for the sins of the whole world, why is not the whole world saved? We can lay aside the Calvinist doctrine of limited atonement for the time being. It is far easier for our earthly minds to comprehend the concept of God's eternal knowledge of things. God knew, beforehand, all those who would accept the sacrifice of Jesus on the cross as the atonement for their salvation.

Understanding this, we can logically argue that not one person today is beyond the scope of the saving grace of God. Jesus died for your sins about two thousand years before you were even born. Nothing you could have possibly done has been a surprise to Him. It is Scripturally obvious that this is true; He died for your sins and if you call upon His grace, He will impart eternal salvation to you.

Yes, salvation is available to even you. No sin is too obnoxious to repel the love of the Savior!

Look at Romans 6:23:

> *"For the wages of sin is death; but the gift of God
> is eternal life through Jesus Christ our Lord."*

We see that salvation from sin is a gift from God. What happens when someone refuses a gift? They don't get it, do they? The Holiness people say that Jesus is a Gentleman Who forces His way on no one. I am sorry Brother Calvin, that is true.

There are those who have so hardened their hearts to the call of the Spirit that they will die in their sins rather than receive the free gift of eternal life. There are still more who, as another old Gospel song reminds us, "Untold millions are still untold."

As an aside, aren't we blessed that God has allowed us to hear these old Gospel songs rather than seeking to anchor our souls in the crashing waves of the storm-tossed culture of the day as blared forth by some of the *Praise Bands* of the modern-day *rock and roll churches* which preach a gospel of the culture of the day rather than living the gospel of the Word of God out into the world of lost humanity?

THE GREAT COMMISSION

Paul asks us several questions in regard to the need for the "Great Commission" from the last chapter of Matthew. Paul speaks in Romans 10: 13-17:

> *" 13 For whosoever shall call upon the name of the
> Lord shall be saved. 14 How then shall they call on
> him in whom they have not believed? And how
> shall they believe in him of whom they have not
> heard? And how shall they hear without a
> preacher? 15 And how shall they preach, except
> they be sent? As it is written, How beautiful are
> the feet of them that preach the gospel of peace,
> and bring glad tidings of good things! 16 But they
> have not all obeyed the gospel. For Esaias saith,
> Lord, who hath believed our report? 17 So then
> faith cometh by hearing, and hearing by the word*

of God."

Jesus said, in what we call "The Great Commission" of Matthew 28: 18-20:

> *" 18 And Jesus came and spake unto them, saying, All power is given unto me in heaven and in earth. 19 Go ye, therefore, and teach all nations, baptizing them in the name of the Father, and of the Son, and of the Holy Ghost: 20 Teaching them to observe all things whatsoever I have commanded you: and, lo, I am with you alway, even unto the end of the world. Amen."*

WHO IS A PREACHER?

Looking at both of these passages, we can consider that the "preacher sent" of whom Paul spoke, is us. We call ourselves the followers of Christ. So, we must consider His directions to us (The word "ye" speaks of a plurality of persons. Therefore, we are included within the group with which He was speaking all those years ago.) as binding upon ourselves. Paul did not mean "preacher" to be considered only as one who stands in front of a group on the Lord's Day. Every single Christian is tasked with the requirement of spreading the message of the Gospel in the "Pulpit of Life."

The two passages, then, speak a personal God-appointed mission field of our own daily concourse among humanity. Consider the importance of this charge: Each Christian is given the awesome privilege of working for, and with, the Creator of the Universe in the spreading of the news about His goal of the salvation of lost sinners.

Consider Luke 19: 10:

> *For the Son of man is come to seek and to save that which was lost.··*

We are asked to take part - with Jesus - in His purpose of sending the message of salvation, for which He died in His humanity on the Cross of Calvary. We are tasked with the commission to take this message out into the created world of mankind.

Paul asks, and answers, a very simple question: "If anyone who calls upon the Lord will be saved, why are so many still not saved?" His answer is very simple: We, the blood-bought Christian, have not followed those simple military-style orders as given in the Great Commission. What poor soldiers of the Cross are we! And, yet, we claim Him as LORD and Savior. We have not properly taken the Words of the Gospel out into the world.

We cannot expect this "sent" preacher to be Satan. Neither can we expect even the holy angels to perform this task. As we read the tenth chapter of Acts, we find the angels instructing Cornelius to find a Christian, Peter in this case, to give forth those words of eternal life.

I submit that these angels were not lazy. They did not possess the complete understanding of the things of human salvation. First Peter 1: 11-12 informs us:

> " [11] *Searching what, or what manner of time the Spirit of Christ which was in them did signify,* [12] *when it testified beforehand the sufferings of Christ, and the glory that should follow. Unto whom it was revealed, that not unto themselves, but unto us they did minister the things which are now reported unto you by them that have preached the gospel unto you with the Holy Ghost sent down from heaven; which things the angels desire to look into.* "

This is not to be considered a lack of cognitive ability on the part of the holy angels. It is rather a holy submission to the God-ordained order of the created universe. God has so ordained that this spreading of the Gospel message is the task of the Blood-bought believer. It is we, you and me, that is to spread the word that Jesus Christ died in time so that vile sinners, such as myself, might live in eternity.

May each of us be faithful to our Heavenly calling. Souls, eternally existent souls, of real men, women, boys and girls, have the eternal destiny of their immortal souls waiting to find the Truth of the message of this Gospel. THAT my friends, is REALITY. That Satan, and Satan inspired men of earth would attempt to thwart our efforts to follow the Lord is to be expected!

OBEDIENCE TO THE LORD

Even beyond that spiritual reality, we are all too often amiss in treating Jesus as The Lord, Who is worthy of being accepted and understood, even as we lie when we call Him Lord! If we are to call ourselves followers of Christ and claim Him as Lord, we must have an interest in that for which He left the hallowed halls of Heaven and came to the muddy hills of earth and the Cross of Calvary.

Is this really important to Him, that we follow His Great Commission? If there is any doubt in your mind about this, read the last sentence of the above paragraph. This is part of the history of the Person of Jesus Christ.

May we be always faithful to our Heavenly calling. We may recall the teaching of Jesus on prayer. Matthew 6:10 is part of this preaching from The Sermon on the Mount. In this verse, as part of the prayer, Jesus said, *"Thy kingdom come, Thy will be done in earth, as it is in heaven."* We know His grace if we are truly Christian. We also know His will concerning our deportment in this world of time. We are to be witnesses of Him and the Gospel Message of salvation. That witness of ours is part of the Gospel Message; that is His chosen means of spreading the message of eternal salvation.

We are never alone in our fidelity to spread that message. We buttress the power and proclamation of that message with prayer that the power of God will go with our faithfulness and witness. Indeed, without the infusion of His power our voicing of the

Gospel is fruitless. We are to be workers *with* Him into the world. This is a point we must always consider. He calls and sends us. Through the prayer of the saints, He will empower those He has sent.

By the way, lest there be any misunderstanding, Biblically, the word "saint" applies to those who are born again by the power of the crucified and resurrected Christ. We are not a special "breed" of humanity. No church council has ever named us as saints. But the power of God resides upon us. If we are to access this power for our daily witness, we must understand that this power is ours to use for Him. Our prayers may not always move mountains, but our prayers can call the Holy Spirit to move the hearts of humans to accept the Lord's salvation.

WE CANNOT GO AGAINST SATAN IN OUR OWN POWER

We do not, cannot, act in our own power as we go against the powers of the wicked one. Read the fourth chapter of Matthew and be impressed to spend much time in the Scripture. Every temptation which Satan thew at Jesus was met by a quotation from the inspired and preserved Words of God. Even when Satan attempted to misuse and misapply the Scripture, one of his favorite ploys to tempt us, he was met with the answer from the true Scripture.

Again, souls of real men, real women, real boys, and real girls have the eternal destiny of their immortal souls waiting to find the Truth of the message of the Gospel. That is a spiritual reality. It is we who are too often amiss in our duty to both God and humanity! *"God so loved the world,"* is the beginning of a precious verse (John 3: 16). If we are to call ourselves followers of Christ and claim Him as Lord, we must have an interest in that for which He left the sinless halls of Heaven and came to the sinful world of man and to the Cross of Calvary.

Calvary was not an accident; it was more than a miscarriage of justice; it is part of the eternal plan of God to offer salvation from sin and peace with God. Our privilege in this is that we are allowed the task of warning and telling others of the great love which God has for them.

Jesus, in His humanity died in time so that others could live in eternity. Consider Revelation13:86:

> *"And all that dwell upon the earth shall worship him,* [This "him" is identified as the Anti-Christ. The narrative so identified this "him" as such.] *whose names are not written in the book of life of the Lamb* ["The Lamb" is, of course, a reference to Jesus as "the Lamb of God." See John 1:29 and 36 to find John the Baptist identify Jesus with these words.] *slain from the foundation of the world."*

The first part of this verse is very "time specific" to the Tribulation era. It is speaks of the sad reality of those who follow the antichrist. But, the last part of the verse is timeless. It speaks of the truth that Jesus was committed to the fact of Calvary even before the world, and the sin of mankind, would necessitate the reality of that cruel cross on the Humanity of the very Son of God.

How can we expect anyone to be saved who does not understand that faith in Jesus is needed to find salvation? Matthew 18:20 makes it obvious that we have been sent to witness of this salvation in Jesus. In an above passage from Romans, chapter ten, Paul says that *not all have obeyed the gospel* (Romans 10:16). Who is that "they?" It isn't the unsaved, in this particular case. Not in totality!

The unsaved? They might not even know about the Great Commission. Even if they were to understand that, they would still not understand the salvation which they've never experienced. Those who Paul says have not obeyed the gospel are us - the Christian who has not carried the message of the Cross into the world of lost humanity.

Most importantly, the unsaved are not sent to bring the words of salvation to the lost. They are on "the other team." They are sinners bound by their sin to Satan. We are the ones called to the task. As Paul put it, *"How shall they go except they be sent?"* We are the ones who have been sent. But we ignore our calling and chase our life as though we were without Christ and His Commission voiced to us.

Yes; salvation is freely given to us. But what kind of gratitude toward Christ for His sacrifice, or compassion to lost humanity for their lost condition, do we show by refusing the simple gift of sharing the truth of Jesus with those of our shared humanity - to speak nothing of what we owe to family, friends, and co-workers?

If faith does come from hearing the Words of God, who would be responsible for not allowing others to hear those eternally inspired and preserved Words of God? It cannot be speaking of the sinner who has never heard the message of salvation. He cannot relate a message he has never heard. We are the ones called to preach, in oratory, simple conversation, and anointed life-style which gives out those words by actions and words of witness, giving out tracts, writing, simply allowing ourselves to be used of God ... It is we who have failed our task.

In our lack, we have horribly failed both God and man!

THE DRONE

Personally, my own style of oratory is so constructed that the United States Army has fashioned a weapon based upon my speaking style. It is "The Drone." I tend to drone on way too long.

The military even has a doctrine of war fashioned after my speaking style. It is called "Shock and Awe." The "shock" is when the people see me. "You mean that 300-pound blob is going to speak to us?" The "Awe" is when they begin to hear me speak. "Awww; is he gonna talk forever?" No, folks, it just seems that I'll be speaking forever!" I am that unexciting as a speaker!

But God has called even me to be a witness before men of the great, eternal grace of Jesus, the Messiah of Israel and the Author of Salvation for all who would respond to His call of Grace and Mercy.

My ability, or rather my lack of ability is not the point. Paul said, of the Gospel message, " ... *for it is the power of God unto salvation to every one that believeth* ... " (Romans 1:16) We are to be faithful as messengers. It is God Who supplies the power to reach an individual unto his, or her, salvation. If we will but do our part, it is certain that He will do His.

CHAPTER 1
THE GROUNDWORK

My chosen subject to write about is that the judgment of God is not coming upon us as a people. **It is here**; at least the beginning of that judgment is here! We have earned it and God is supplying it upon us. That was my professed title. I am going to assume that you must have concluded that my title had nothing to do with my thesis as presented.

Not so. I have been laying a sort of groundwork by explaining our duty within the Gospel as being part of the "church age." Our "assigned task" in this world is the spread the Truth that Jesus Christ died in time so that others could live in eternity. That is our first duty as Christians in this world of time.

It is important that we understand that the United States is not, never has been, and never could be a "covenant people" before the Lord. Our Constitution, however, has granted us a guarantee of freedom of religion. Nowhere does the phrase exist in that constitution of a freedom *from* religion. Those who argue for this are guilty of attempting to establish a *new* religion. They expect that the Government would use their view to establish a new religious perspective.

They may argue that five-and six-year-olds singing Christmas Carols at a kindergarten assembly are guilty of establishing a religion. Maybe someone should tell them that the Christian *religion* pre-dates, by many centuries, the foundation of this nation. That religion even pre-dates the founding of our *"Mother County,"* Great Britain. It is they, not the young children, who are attempting to establish a new religion of Secular Humanism as the sole power among the religions of the nation.

A CHRISTIAN NATION

We can go back and hear the original words of Patriot Patrick

Henry. He said:

> "An appeal to arms and the God of hosts is all that is left to us. But we shall not fight our battle alone. There is a just God that presides over the destinies of nations. The battle sir, is not to the strong alone. Is life so dear or peace so sweet as to be purchased at the price of chains and slavery? Forbid it almighty God. I know not what course others may take, but as for me, give me liberty, or give me death."

I would like to note that this quotation was found in a tract from the Pilgrim Tract Society Inc, PO Box 126. Randleman, NC 27317, USA. It is amazing to consider how much information is packed into this small four-page tract: "THE 'FORSAKEN ROOTS' OF OUR COUNTY: The United States of America." It would be well worth your effort to order a supply of these tracts for use in your own personal work.

This brings me to the only complaint I have with this tract: there is insufficient space to affix a stamp for the church name when these are passed out. Not only is this a good way to advertise for our churches, it is also a hedge against someone going to the church down the street where the Bible may not be proclaimed!

Those many years younger than myself may have never heard that speech in its context. We have begun to remove many references to the God of history as we seek to redefine our own history.

"... in 1892. (Supreme Court) justice Josiah David Brewster, writing in *Church of the Holy Trinity vs. U.S.* the unanimous supreme Court decision which has never been overturned, held as matter of law, of fact, and of history that. ..

> *"This is a Christian nation ... ,"*

This is akin to a simple sandwich of knowledge. Go to www.firstprinciplespress.org for the entire smorgasbord of fact which they have laid out for us.

THE BIBLE IS THE WORD OF GOD

There is more. I found in my file's copies of a 1983 appeal in which a joint session of congress held that the Bible is the Word of God. Furthermore, President Ronald Reagan proclaimed, again 1983, as "The Year of the Bible."

I would assume that I received this in the mail in either late 1982 or in 1983. I honestly. have no recall as to when, or from whom, I received this. It is, however, a fact of history that the Congress of the United States, in joint session, did declare the Bible to be the Word of God. As a corollary of this fact, then President Ronald Reagan proclaimed 1983 as "The Year of the Bible."

There is more. How often have we heard politicians ending speeches with the words, "God bless America," or "so help me, God."

We have covered actions by the Supreme Court of the United States, both houses of the United States Congress, and the President of the United States affirming our allegiance to the Bible and the God Who gave it.

We are not a covenant people. But we are a people who have, by the three primary branches of our national government, vowed vows unto God. Since we, as a nation and a people, have made such vows to God, we have seen His hand of blessing fall upon us often in our National life.

These are signs of vows we have voiced to the Lord of Glory.

Several times presidents have proclaimed national days of petition to the God of Scripture. We have given great freedoms to other, often false in my eyes, religions in the name of Freedom of Religion. Read the Bible through, pay special attention to the words of Moses and the prophets to find the attitude of God towards those who have vowed fidelity to God and yet have gone on to honor false religions and false gods even as they departed from the worship and respect for, and to, the True God of nations and Creation.

For us to supply less than our best for that Heavenly Master, shows us to be unprofitable "angels" unto the Lord. The word "Angel" as almost all of those here know, simply means "Messenger." As we have stated previously in this paper, we have a Message of eternal consequence to take into the world.

TEARS IN HEAVEN

The Bible does inform us that there will be tears in Heaven. (Revelation 7: 17 and Isaiah 23: 8) I would believe that, primarily, these are tears of joy. But there will also be tears of regret when we see just how poorly we have served our Heavenly Master. The joy of Heaven will be full. The regrets of Heaven will become soon vanished from our lives by the loving Hand of God.

I must note that the above governmental actions were performed by men and women who sat as our representatives. Therefore, this must be considered as our own actions. WE have made solemn vows to God. Can we honestly argue that these vows have been paid? Rather, must we argue that we have spoken and vowed lies unto the Lord of All?

Instead, has not our nation flaunted sin in the face of God? Ancient Israel and Judah did not always have Godly kings. They had kings that led them into gross idolatry and false worship. These two kingdoms were judged for their national sins. How much more are we guilty of failing to live unto God after we have pledged a fidelity to Him? We have not done this under kings. We have done this under the representatives we have elected as our leaders!

POLITICAL REALITIES

I do not often mention political realities when I preach or write. But we do need to exercise great care when we cast our votes. And, as a representative democracy, I do believe that it is a duty, under God, to cast our votes in His will.

We have seen several examples of request, by the people's (us) representatives, that this nation be treated as though it were a covenant people of God. Be careful of that for which you ask with your vote! It is important to note, once again, that the United States population is not a covenant people. We never could be. The only Covenant People mentioned in Scripture are the people of Abraham, Isaac and Jacob.

Neither are we, or any nation on earth, a Christian Nation. Christianity is not a group exercise. It is based on a heart response of individuals. People are Christians, or they are not. Nations may have a predisposition toward a Christian cultural view. But nations are not Christian, as concerning salvation.

After all of our protestations about our being a Christian nation, can we even claim such a predisposition toward a Christian cultural view? Is it not true that we live in a political society which claims a need to be on the "right side of history?" Folks, there is a more important side. We have so tipped our Ship of State that we now list towards the wrong side of eternity.

CHAPTER 2
PROPHECY

Many years ago, my wife and I traveled to a nearby city to hear a speaker talk on matters of prophecy. This was about 1980. The speaker made a preposterous claim. He said that, according to his view of prophecy, the Soviet Union would need to fall. He said that there was a clause in the constitution of the U.S.S.R. which forbid religion. He continued, since there will be a one-world church, under Anti-Christ, the U.S.S.R. must fall and be replaced with a system which will look more favorably on religious expression.

Further. he added, even though the U.S.S.R. must fall, it is obvious, from prophecy, that they will remain a world power. (I did not put any of the speaker's words in quotation marks. These words are paraphrased from my memory.)

In that same vein, my own view of prophecy would argue that the United States must fall from our perch atop the "'food chain" of nations. I have never found any hint of the United States in any prophecy of Scripture. The real power seems to reside in Europe. Russia is a power, although her planned invasion of Israel will fail as God destroys her, and her allies, armies. There will be an oriental power- my guess (and it is only that!) is that this will be China.

After the dust from this time of *"Jacob's Trouble"* (Jeremiah 30:7) settles, the only power on earth will be Israel as she sees Her King Messiah on the throne. He will justly judge the nations of the earth. Of His reign there will be no end in the history of this world.

KING OF KINGS

Kings and kingdoms will have come and gone. King Jesus will be Lord, and King, forever! God gave king Nebuchadnezzar a dream concerning the history of the world. Daniel, God's prophet, told the tale of this history.

> *And in the days of these kings shall the God of heaven set up a kingdom which shall never be destroyed: and the kingdom shall not be left to other people, but it shall break in pieces and consume all these kingdoms, and it shall stand for ever, forasmuch as thou sawest that the stone was cut of the mountain without hands, and that it brake in pieces the iron, the brass, the clay, the silver, and the gold; the great God hath made known to the king what shall come to pass hereafter: and the dream is certain, and the interpretation thereof sure." (Daniel 2:44-45)*

When we speak of the prophecy of God, we are simply speaking of certain history which has not yet happened.

COVENANT PEOPLE

What does the Bible say about the true Covenant people of God? I would note a significant difference in their covenant status and our assumed status as proclaimed by our vows of fidelity to the Lord. We have made pronouncements of fidelity. Those true Covenant People have received promises directly given from God. We may be honor-bound by our own words; they are bound by the Honor of the Words of God!

ABRAHAM

Of Abraham God has said:

> *"And I will make of thee a great nation, and I will bless thee, and make thy name great: and thou shalt be a blessing." Genesis 12:2*

Also Genesis 17:4-6; 18:18; 22:17; 24:35 (A servant of Abraham describes the material blessings which God has bestowed upon Abraham.); 28:4; 46:3; First Kings 3:8; Galatians 3:14. Note that this is only a representative list of the blessings of God upon Abraham. It is not the full list of available references to the blessings of God upon Abraham!

ISAAC

Of Isaac, God has said. Genesis 21:12-13,

> *[12] And God said unto Abraham, Let it not be grievous in thy sight because of the lad,* [Ishmael being sent away. See verse ten.] *and because of thy bondwoman; in all that Sarah hath said unto thee, hearken unto her voice; for in Isaac shall thy seed be called. [13] And also of the son of the bondwoman will I make a nation, because he is thy seed."*

(Note that God said that of Ishmael He will make a nation. The promise is not to make a covenant people of Ishmael; "in Isaac shall thy seed be called.")

It is instructive to include Genesis 25: 19 at this point:

> *"And these are the generations of Isaac, Abraham's son: Abraham begat Isaac."*

It is a fine line of distinction, but a certain line. Isaac is the son of Abraham, thus the inheritor of the Promises of God. Of Ishmael, it is only considered that he is the "seed" of Abraham. He is not listed in the listing of Abraham's generations as to the promises of faith and Covenant.

As for presuming to include Ishmael among the spiritual descendants of Abraham as considering the covenants, simply because Ishmael is the physical "seed" of Abraham: In such a situation we would be compelled to include the physical sons of Keturah, Abraham's second wife after the death of Sarah. These can be read about in the 25th chapter of Genesis. We read. in Genesis 25:6 that these sons were sent away from Isaac, as Ishmael had been sent away after the birth of Isaac.

In light of these facts. and the general outline of the Bible, it is best that we consider the Words of God concerning the linage of the promises of the Covenant people. Of Ishmael, we do read that he returned to assist Isaac in the burying of their father. We never read that he was considered as an "heir to the promises.

29

"Of Ishmael, it is said that God would bless him, making him *"a nation."* Notice that this is not a nation of blessing. The blessing, and the covenant of blessing, was the right of the son of Abraham and Sarah. Isaac, a son of the old age of both Sarah and Abraham was a supernatural birth. Ishmael was a purely physical birth.

Without doing any violence to the Scriptural record, we could extrapolate that the *religion* of Isaac is spiritual and reaching into the supernatural of God's plan for the ages: that is the Messiah of our salvation. Meanwhile, the *religion* of Ishmael, is only of natural importance. It does not reach the Heaven of Divine favor; nor does it lead to eternal salvation.

Of Jacob the son of Isaac, the Bible does argue that Jacob was a "son of the promise." Genesis 35:10-12

> *" 10 And God said unto him, Thy name is Jacob: thy name shall not be called any more Jacob, but Israel shall be thy name: and he called his name Israel. 11 And God said unto him, I am God Almighty: be fruitful and multiply; a nation and a company of nations shall be of thee, and kings shall come out of thy loins; 12 And the land which I gave Abraham and Isaac, to thee I will give it, and to thy seed after thee will I give the land."*

In this passage the promises given to Abraham were confirmed as passed on to Isaac and Jacob.

I believe that it is Genesis 12:3 which gives the true reason for the many blessings placed upon the people of the United States:

> *"And I will bless them that bless thee, and curse him that curseth thee: and in thee shall all the families of the earth be blessed."*

This was, and is, part of the blessing which God promised to Abraham and his descendants.

For the most part, the people of this land have given a certain respect and human-rights protections to the people of Abraham. For much of this time those children of Abraham had not found the rest of the world so hospitable.

THE NEW WORLD

In 1492, as Christopher Columbus sailed out of Spain in his voyage to the "New World," there were many other boats fleeing Spain. This flotilla of displaced persons were Jews who had been ordered to depart from Spain. My understanding is that many, if not most, of these Jews had no idea where they were to go. They had just been ordered to depart under pain of severe persecution and the likelihood of death should they not depart. Spain had found its own version of a "final solution."

The "New World," popularized by the voyage of Columbus, was generally hospitable to these often-persecuted Jews. Generally speaking, they were welcomed by the English colonies. As His Covenant People were blessed, so did God bless those who blessed them. This is the real reason for the many blessingS which God has given this nation.

SHADOWS OF PERSECUTION

Of late this has been slowly changing. This is why the shadows of the persecution of God have begun to cast their forms before them onto our national stage.

Make note of the final clause of the above verse from Genesis, *"all the families of the earth be blessed."* God promised to bless the entire world through the efforts of Abraham's descendants through his son, Isaac. It seems as though every issue of the magazine, "Israel My Glory," contains news articles telling of medical and other advances through the genius of the Jewish people of Israel.

Whether it be the arts, science, medicine, and even sports, a short look will give evidence to the fact that the Jewish presence rises far above the miniscule percentage of the Jewish population within the world. The greatest blessing of Israel to the nations of the world is, of course, that through Israel came the Messiah, Jesus Christ, the Lord of Salvation!

THE DAVIDIC COVENANT

The next covenant we must consider is the Davidic Covenant. Now I understand the first objection to including this in our list. "But this does not consider the former covenants; the former covenants were all with the people of Abraham, Isaac and Jacob." But this covenant does consider these same people. It is connected with their earthly government - the King of Israel.

The well-known Scofield Reference Bible (Scofield Reference Bible, The; Rev. Dr. C. I. Scofield, D.D .. editor; Copyright: Oxford University Press, Inc.; 1909, 1917, 1937, 1945. New York, NY.) has been accessed in this portion of our study.

Beginning in the seventh chapter of Second Samuel we find David reflecting on the great mercy which the Lord has shed upon him. In this spirit David tells the prophet Nathan that he wishes to show his thanks to God by building a Temple in Jerusalem. Nathan said, essentially. "O.K. God is with you in this desire."

Next, we are reminded that it is always good to seek the will of the Lord before we presume to speak in His Name. We pick up the story in the fifth verse of this seventh chapter of Second Samuel. We continue through verse seventeen.

> *5 Go and tell my servant David, Thus saith the LORD, Shalt thou build me an house for me to dwell in? 6 Whereas I have not dwelt in any house since the time that I brought up the children of Israel out of Egypt, even to this day, but have walked in a tent and in a tabernacle. 7 In all the places wherein I have walked with all the children of Israel spake I a word with any of the tribes of Israel, whom I commanded to feed my people Israel, saying, Why build ye not me an house of cedar? 8 Now therefore so shalt thou say unto my*

servant David, Thus saith the LORD of hosts, I took thee from the sheepcote, from following the sheep, to be ruler over my people, over Israel: [9] *And I was with thee whithersoever thou wentest. and have cut off all thine enemies out of thy sight and have made thee a great name. like unto the name of the great men that are in the earth.* [10] *Moreover I will appoint a place for my people Israel, and will plant them, that they may dwell in a place of their own, and move no more; neither shall the children of wickedness afflict them any more, as beforetime,* [11] *And as since the time that I commanded judges to be over my people Israel, and have caused thee to rest from all thine enemies. Also the LORD telleth thee that he will make thee an house.* [12] *And when thy days be fulfilled, and thou shalt sleep with thy fathers, I will set up thy seed after thee, which shall proceed out of thy bowels, and I will establish his kingdom.* [13] *He shall build an house for my name, and I will stablish the throne of his kingdom for ever.* [14] *I will be his father, and he shall be my son. If he commit iniquity, I will chasten him with the rod of men, and with the stripes of the children of men:* [15] *But my mercy shall not depart away from him, as I took it from Saul, whom I put away before thee.* [16] *And thine house and thy kingdom shall be established for ever before thee:* [17] *According to all these words, and according to all this vision, so did Nathan speak unto David."*

God made several distinct promises concerning David and his royal seed in relation to Israel. The people of Israel right now, at this present time, do reside in the land which God has given to them. Is this the final regathering of Israel? Are the events of The Land prepared for the end time events? There may yet be another dispersal and another regathering. But we must note that the physical stage is now set, as it is, for the fulfillment of the end-times prophecies!

I would not presume to know all of the events of the end times. I do believe that the end is close. With ancients from another day, I must say "Maranatha. Even so, come Lord Jesus."

With this groundwork of the coming Messiah of Israel, or to be more correct, the coming reappearance of this Messiah, and His relationship to the Davidic Covenant. we must now consider the concept of the final covenant that we will consider: The New Covenant.

Before we get into the New Covenant, I must note that Scofield finds and comments upon, five covenants affected by the Davidic Covenant.

> "(l)   A Davidic 'house'; i.e., posterity, family.
>
> (2)   A 'throne'; royal authority.
>
> (3)   A kingdom; i.e., sphere of rule.
>
> (4)   In perpetuity: 'for ever.'
>
> "(5) And this fourfold covenant has but one condition: disobedience in the Davidic family is to be visited with chastisement. but not to the abrogation of the covenant (2 Sam. 7.15; Psa. 89.20-37; Isa. 24.5; 54.3). The chastisement fell: first in the division of the kingdom under Rehoboam, and, finally in the captivities (2 Ki. 25.1-7). Since that time but one King of the Davidic family has been crowned at Jerusalem and He was crowned with thorns."

In Thy Kingdom Come (Biblical Study of the Kingdom of God, A): Showers, Jim and Katulka, Chris, General Editors; Friends of Israel Gospel Ministry, Inc,; Bellmawr, NJ 08099; 2019, in an article, "God's Kingdom and the Davidic Covenant" (Written by Tom Simcox) there are five notations made concerning the Davidic Covenant.

> "1.   I will appoint a place for my people Israel, and will plant them, that they may dwell in a place of their own and move no more.
>
> 2.   I will set up your seed after you.

3.   I will establish his kingdom.

4.   I will establish the throne of his kingdom forever.

5.   Your house and your kingdom shall be established forever."

There is no discrepancy between these two views. Schofield is completely correct in his historical view of the outworking of the kingdom under David's physical son, Solomon. Simcox is also completely correct in his view, taken from the pre-history of prophecy. The Messiah, Jesus, is the ultimate son of David. The genealogy of Joseph, the "step-father" of Jesus, from the Book of Matthew, gives to Jesus the legal right to the throne of David. The genealogy of Mary, as given in the Book of Luke, further establishes the physical lineage of Jesus as a "son of David."

THE NEW COVENANT

As we consider the New Covenant. we are compelled to consider the Truth of Messiah, Jesus, in relation to this "New Covenant" for it is the "New Testament of His Blood" (Matthew 26:28) that gives the power and reality of this "New Covenant."

This will be the final covenant we will consider. This is the most important of the covenants as it touches upon the "New Birth" of which Jesus spoke in the third chapter of John. Jesus announced the commencement of this new covenant during his institution of what we now call the "communion service." This is a time we celebrate the fact of His atoning death on the Cross of Calvary. After passing out the bread Jesus offered the cup. He said:

> *"This cup is the new testament in my blood, which is shed for you." (Luke 22:20)*

The word "testament," of course, means "covenant." Thus, Jesus was speaking of the establishment of this new covenant.

This was not a new concept in the ears of these disciples. They had been seeped in the Words of the Old Testament prophets. Scofield places his notes on the New Covenant upon Hebrews 8:8. I would like to include the passage starting with the fifth verse and continuing to the end of the chapter - verse 13. of this eighth chapter of Hebrews. The passage begins with a short review of the Old Testament priest of the Law.

5 Who serve unto the example and shadow of heavenly things. as Moses was admonished of God when he was about to make the tabernacle: for, See, saith he, that thou make all things according to the pattern shewed to thee in the mount. 6 But now hath he (Jesus - as the full context indicates.) *obtained a more excellent ministry, by how much also he is the mediator of a better covenant, which was established upon better promises. 7 For if that first covenant had been faultless, then should no place have been sought for the second. 8 For finding fault with the, he saith, Behold, the days come, saith the Lord, when I will make a new covenant with the house of Israel and with the house of Judah. 9 Not according to the covenant that I made with their fathers in the day when I took them by the hand to lead them out of the land of Egypt; because they continued not in my covenant, and I regarded them not, saith the Lord. 10 For this is the covenant that I will make with the house of Israel after those days, saith the Lord: I will put my laws into their mind, and write them in their hearts: and I will be to them a God, and they shall be to me a people. 11 And they shall not teach every man his neighbor, and every man his brother, saying, Know the Lord: for all shall know me, from the least to the greatest. 12 For I will be merciful to their unrighteousness, and their sins and their iniquities will I remember no more. 13 In that time he saith, A new covenant. he hath made the first old. Now that which decayeth and waxeth old is ready to vanish away."*

The human penman of Hebrews had accessed Jeremiah 31:31-34 in this passage:

> ³¹ *Behold, the days come, saith the LORD, that I will make a new covenant with the house of Israel, and with the house of Judah.* ³² *Not according to the covenant that I made with their fathers in the day that I took them by the hand to bring them out of the land of Egypt, which my covenant they brake, although I was an husband unto them, saith the LORD.* ³³ *But this shall be the covenant that I will make with the house of Israel; After those days, saith the LORD, I will put my law in their inward parts, and write it in their hearts; and will be their God, and they shall be my people.* ³⁴ *And they shall teach no more every man his neighbour, and every man his brother, saying Know the LORD: for they shall all know me, from the least of them unto the greatest of them, saith the LORD: for I will forgive their iniquity, and I will remember their sin no more."*

The point being made as concerns this "New Covenant" is that this is a promise made to the Jew as were the other covenants. This covenant, however, is part of the blessing to the entire world through the people of Abraham. This covenant is one in which we do share with the Jewish people. It is the covenant of salvation, based on the shed blood of Jesus, and our faith in the blood sacrifice of the humanity of the very Son of God.

It is this upon which our faith as Christians is predicated.

A TWO-FOLD PURPOSE

The rather lengthy session on the covenants had a two-fold purpose:

First, this illustrates that this nation is not a covenant people of God. We have made certain vows to God but are not a Covenant People of His.

Second, we have seen a shift within our national conscience of late in which we have lost our understanding of the Jewishness of the covenants of God. They remain His *special* people on this earth. We live in the *Time* of *the Gentiles,* dispensationally. But the Jewish people remain as *His Covenant People* and are the holders of many of the promises of God. They, indeed, are the focus of the end times event we, theologically, call the Great Tribulation. The Bible (Jeremiah 30:7) refers to this time as *The Time of Jacob's trouble.*

THE GREAT TRIBULATION & KINGDOM AGE

This great end-times event ushers in the Kingdom Age of Messiah's rule. This one-thousand- year reign of Messiah will see the end of this present period of time and continue into the times of eternity where the rule of the Lord continues through-out eternity.

Before this eventuality will come, of course, the Great Tribulation Era must occur. However this, in turn, is preceded by the rapture of the church. The rapture is the next great event in the calendar of God's rule over this earth.

CHAPTER 3

THE UNITED STATES NOT MENTIONED IN PROPHECY

Since the United States is not mentioned in "end times" prophecy, it would seem that our demise as a world power will proceed the rapture. This is not necessary for God's time-table to be completed, but it does seem somehow to be obvious to any end time scenario as set forth in Scripture.

This would not be the first time that a regional, or even a world, power fell under the judgment of God. The sins of the land of Canaan were judged in the giving of that land to the people of Jacob. These people, first the northern kingdom of Israel and then the southern kingdom of Judah, were also judged for their sins and, in turn, fell. The difference between these two groups is that the People of Jacob are the Covenant People of God and will be regathered to retain their place in the Plan of God.

It is a fact of Scripture and history that nations have risen to great prominence as God has used them for His purposes. They have begun to deny, or ignore Him and have been replaced. We see this over and over again. God sets up kingdoms and then removes them in testament to His power and glory. We are no different in this ebb and flow of sinful humanities social and political progress and egress on the stage of humanities actions.

We have seen an upsurge of a religion which misapplies the covenant promises of God. This is a great national sin as it substitutes a false God for the True and Living God. Does this mean that this religion should not have a place at the table of ideas in our land? Of course not; this nation is founded on a principle of freedom of religion. Any attempt to disenfranchise one religion is to risk the same theory to settle on all religions. This freedom gives us free reign to legally, even under the law of man, perform our duties to the Lord as cited in Scripture. If only we would begin to use this freedom of man to preach the true spiritual freedom of God!

In times of conflict, we ought always to obey the laws of God as concern's our witness. His Law is spiritual and eternal. Man's law sits on a lower plain. It can only consider the earthly passions of sinful humanity.

> *"And fear not them which kill the body, but are not able to kill the soul: but rather fear him which is able to destroy both soul and body in hell."* (Matthew 10:28)

Rather than proscribe this religion we must realize that the individuals thereof are lost sinners, as were we before we found salvation in the Lord. What is needed, instead of hostility, is honest evangelism. This cannot be a hostile message. True Christian evangelism is an exercise of friendship and loving acceptance. We may consider the instruction of Jesus from John 8:10-11:

> *"When Jesus had lifted up himself, and saw none but the woman, where are those thine accusers? Hath no man condemned thee? She said, No man, Lord. And Jesus said unto her, Neither do I condemn thee, go, and sin no more."*

Note that He DID call her FROM her sin. Never forget this fact.

The Law, under which her original accusers had brought her before Jesus, demanded the both the man and the woman were guilty. Where was the man? The purpose, obviously, had not been a zeal for the Law, but an attempt to tempt Jesus. Rome did not allow the Jewish leaders the right to execute criminals. That is the reason that Jesus was led to Pilate. The haters needed the permission of Rome to execute Him.

There have always been those who wish to use the tenants of

their religious understanding to do evil. We even have those who claim to follow Jesus that would pervert His Words to prosecute their own agenda.

I cannot remember the name of the movie. At one point, a group of Christians have been brought before the authorities. This movie was set during the tribulation era, so these were people who had sought out the Lord in a time of great hatred and tribulation. One of this group of Christians said, to the one who had betrayed them, "Sandy, I thought that you were a Christian!" Sandy said, "Oh, Patty, anyone can say that they are a Christian."

There are several identifications of a true, Biblical Christian. Matthew - 5:44:

> *"But I say unto you, Love your enemies, bless them that curse you, do good to them that hate you, and pray for them which despitefully use you, and persecute you."*

We have already accessed the Great Commission from Matthew 28. No place in the new covenant of salvation is there any plea to harm others. The Biblical program is not to destroy the unbeliever. The call is to enjoin them to take part in the same salvation as we have found.

Those who ignore the above are not Biblical Christians. They don't even use the same vocabulary of submission to Jesus as should a Biblical Christian. We only have a commission to win the lost. We have no freedom to whip, or harm, them. Such is a counter consideration to the entire purpose of the Christian on this earth.

We have spoken of this truth in large measure earlier in this correspondence. Even if we were to "lose our heads" in the endeavor, our purpose as Christians is to lead the way to the True Savior of the World.

Above all, we must continue to find ways to keep our voices active in the propagation of the message of the gospel. We take our cue from the Words of Jesus, as noted above and from the actions and example of the early church, especially the apostles of our Lord, Jesus Christ.

> " [27] And when they had brought them, and set them before the council: and the high priest asked them, [28] Saying, Did not we straitly command you that ye should not teach in the name? and, behold, ye have filled Jerusalem with your doctrine, and intend to bring this man's blood upon us. [28] Then Peter and the other apostles answered and said, We ought to obey God rather than men." (Acts 5:27-29)

If the next few verses are read, we will find that these apostles immediately began to preach the gospel message in Jesus' Name. This council was the ruling council, under Rome of course, of the people. The high priest was the head of the council. Nevertheless, these men continued to preach the gospel of Jesus. Their duty toward God was more important than any duty to the temporal rulers. We stand in that same situation.

It is not legal to attempt to silence us. The Constitution of the United States gives us the right to practice our religion. Part of that religious practice is to give witness to the fact that Jesus Christ died in time so that we can live in eternity. I can foresee a time when some governmental edict will be used to still our voice. Brethren, we have a duty before the Lord of the Universe, to give forth our voice to relay the message that salvation is of the Lord. We must not be silent. We cannot be silent.

THE REASON FOR JUDGMENT

To allow our voices to be silenced is to sin against the known will of the Lord. This nation now stands under the judgment of God because of our national, and personal sins. We have listed some of those sins above. We stand as a profane people who have vowed to be a pious people. This makes our national sins all the more heinous. We have broken our solemn vows to the Lord of the universe.

As mentioned several times previously, the United States is not listed as among the powers upon the earth in the "end times" prophecies. The real power seems to reside in Europe. Russia remains a world power capable of gathering a group of nations to wage a war against Israel. This will fail as God intervenes to save Israel. The Russian armies, and those of her allies, will be supernaturally destroyed by the Hand of God.

THE ANTICHRIST

The antichrist then brokers a peace accord with Israel guaranteeing them safe passage among their neighbors. It may be that this has to do with the destroyed armies from the earlier invasion. Those Arab neighbors may have been so decimated by their defeat that there is no one able to accost Israel. It may be at this time that Israel restores her ancient Temple because of this power vacuum.

Whatever happens, it seems that the U. S. is reduced to only watching this on our television sets. We have been replaced as a world power by the Europeans. God has removed our status of a world power.

In this we are reminded of the spiritual principle of Daniel 2:21:

> *"And he changeth the times and the seasons: he [God] removeth kings, and setteth up kings: he giveth wisdom unto the wise, and knowledge to them that know understanding."*

We can look at the history of this nation and see the Hand of God blessing us over and over again. We see this from Valley Forge to Pearl Harbor. Yes, even at Pearl Harbor we can see the Hand of God protecting our nation. With all of the destruction, the "dry docks," where the wounded ships could go for repairs, were not touched. Even our stores of fuel were not destroyed; in the great destruction, the seeds of future success and ultimate victory were not spent.

In what manner have our sins separated us from the good favor of God? For one thing, a major thing, we have been decimated by pestilence. In our military, so many of our troops have felt the sting of the pandemic, that we could probably not deploy a large force where they might be needed.

OUR ECONOMY

Our economy has been weakened to an extent probably never seen in our history as "social distancing" has closed many businesses. The fall-out from this is beginning to be displayed by less on the shelf even at our grocery stores. Those few still working are in danger of contracting this disease from their customers. Those not working are being bolstered by unemployment checks to keep foreclosure from putting them out of their homes.

How long can this continue?

In order to help, the government has sent money to support the faltering economy as well as passing laws to criminalize those very foreclosures. This has hurt those who depend on regular rent payments to support their own families. Meanwhile the massive government payments to the general population have caused a skyrocketing national debt to spiral to dizzying heights. At the same time, the great number of people on the unemployment rolls will cause the internal revenue service to collect much less to be used to "pay down" that debt.

Indeed, the only thing holding up the value of the "mighty dollar," is the green ink in the government printing presses.

In politics, we are a much-divided nation. Our society has not seen this type of division since the 1860's. The "winners" in the last election have ousted the former ruling class. Those winners are now set to punish the losers with "show trials." This will probably cause even greater social upheaval even as the mantra of "unity" fills the air.

This is the Hand of God's power upon the affairs of mankind. Let us never forget this truth. As Biblical Christians, we hold a dual citizenship. We are subjects of our nation even as we are children of the God of Heaven. We owe the best we have to both of these entities.

Recall the verse, above, from Daniel 2:21. It is God Who ultimately removes, and sets up kings, or rulers. Whether we are pleased, or dismayed, by the last national election, it is the Hand of God which has determined the winners and the losers. Our duty is to be the best, and most supportive, citizens of our rulers. We support them until they begin to restrict our constitutional, and Godly rights as citizens of Heaven.

That has not happened, yet. We stand as loyal citizens of the ruler God has placed "on the throne." Whether we voted for them, or not, is not the issue. The issue is that they are the choice of God for these times.

> *"Let every soul be subject unto the higher powers. For there is no power but of God: the powers that be are ordained of God. Whosoever therefore resisteth the power resisteth the ordinance of God: and they that resist shall receive to themselves damnation."* (Romans 13:1-2)

This is not to be seen as any form of defeatism. This is to be seen, as it is, a holy subjection to the Person of God.

Nonetheless, we must also consider the realities of prophecy. I believe that we are seeing the beginning of the disfavor of God upon our nation. It is He who has the power to both remove and set up kings (rulers). As our nation is not found in the prophecies of the "end times" of the present epoch of history, it is the

45

providence of God to remove our high situation and prepare the world for the time of "Jacob's Trouble."

OUR CHRISTIAN RESPONABILITY

As Christians, what is our purpose and responsibility during this time of decline?

In Jeremiah 5:25, God laid out the purpose of the coming judgment. The concept was well illustrated in an old *"Dennis the Menace"* comic strip. The one I want to mention is probably from the early 1960's. In this comic Dennis has a large lemonade stand. On this stand is a large sign which reads – "You can have all the lemonade you can drink for five cents." Mr. Wilson, the neighbor of Dennis, is seen handing his cup back to Dennis as he says, "Who says this is all I can drink?" Dennis answers, "I said so! You've already a full cup. That's all you can drink!"

That brings up another old story. Hey! I am an old person and old people tell too many stories, Besides, I said earlier that I "drone" on too much. It was the early 70's.

Suddenly realizing how old I am; it was the 1970's. I had been off active duty in the military for a few weeks. Linda and I were raising our small daughter. Amy *was* pretty young at the time. We had found the perfect babysitter for the few hours before and after school so Linda could return to the job she had held when we were married. Linda loved sewing and this was a small clothing company.

The prospective *baby-sitter* was a family friend that lived across the street from my parents. More importantly this same family had cared for my sister's small children while she worked at a local factory. God knows the beginning and the end. It is amazing to consider how many times such fortuitous situations have "fallen into our laps" simply because God cares for His Own children an often-miraculous manner!

Linda's employment turned out to be very needful later on. I didn't know, at that time, that Agent Orange had somehow weakened my heart. This became very evident starting in the mid-1980's and continuing on. Linda never complained as she was forced to become the primary "breadwinner" for the family.

Now, I've said all the above to give some background on the next story. From this story will come an application concerning how to live a life for Christ into the world of men.

We are back again into the mid-1970's. It was my turn to cook the evening meal. I was "slaving" over a hot store and a large bowl of chili. As Linda came in the door, coming home from work, the telephone was ringing. This is "pre-pocket sized" phones. It is the large phone hanging under a window in the kitchen.

As Linda concluded the phone call, she came over to the counter near where I was preparing our evening meal. Linda asked me, "Where is my plant fertilizer?"

"I haven't seen it."

Then she took on her "wife dumbfounded by husband's stupidity" voice. "It's in the trash. Why did you throw it in the trash?"

"The only thing I've thrown in the trash was the empty can of chili powder."

"Was it this can," Linda said as she held the offending and empty can under my nose.

"Yes," I said, "the chili powder. I put the entire can in. There wasn't much left in it. I really thought we had more."

"Did you read the can before you used it?"

"I know what a can of chili powder looks like. I don't need to

THE JUDGMENT OF GOD UPON AMERICA

read every time I use it."

"You should have read this one. This can says, 'plant fertilizer for small indoor plants.'" I had lost another argument with my wife. Not only that; I also had to pay for a catered meal from Domino's.

I tried to cover by noting that men make the best chefs because we are not afraid to experiment.

Linda just said, "Who says that men make the best chefs?"

I would have said, "I said that men make the best chefs." Unfortunately, I was already out of the kitchen and hiding in front of the T.V. No more arguments tonight after that last one. "Hey, Linda; can you call Domino's and order pizza for tonight?"

"Gladly," she crowed!

CHAPTER 4
OUR NATIONAL SINS

We might get back to this story some time. But first, what are some of the sins for which the nation is being judged. The ancient prophets of Israel certainly seemed bound to follow the rule of "the curse will not causeless come" as they detailed the sins for which their kingdoms were being judged. In what manner have we brought the judgement of God upon ourselves?

One of our national sins was created by the very same institution, the Supreme Court, which had once declared that the U. S. was a Christian nation. The decision mandating the *right* or same-sex marriage unions has caused massive confiscatory judicial judgements over those who have tried to live out their own, supposedly Constitutionally guaranteed, religious freedoms.

Couples have sometimes sought out those who might be unwilling to take part in such marriages and ask them to do just that with their occupations or ministries. When the refusal was voiced, cries of "harassment" and "bigotry" were raised. Not just clergy, but also bakeries, florists, wedding photographers, and of course, ministers [and their churches] have then felt the sting of haters who have not been able to see the right of refusal as anything but discriminatory rather than principled adherence to heartfelt religious duty.

The following is a reasoned approach from the Christian religion, and of course the Biblical view, from which I have refused to perform all marriage in order to protect myself, and the churches I once pastored, from such predatory practitioners. This is from a 20-page, 8 and ½ by 5 and ½ inch, booklet I had authored: *"Same Sex Marriage – A Biblical Perspective."* This was prepared for use as a Bible Conference; I did not use it at that conference as I found more beneficial projects to address.

SAME SEX MARRIAGE: A BIBLICAL CONSIDERATION

"Greetings in the Name of the Lord Jesus Christ. It is under His eternal rule we sit in the counsels of the Godly. It is under His eternal rule we must walk as citizens of Heaven. It is under His eternal rule that we must abide.

"It is said that one day God visited the Garden and found Adam eating a part of the forbidden fruit. 'Didn't I tell you not to do that?' God asked of Adam.

"Adam's reply was, 'But, Lord, everyone else is doing it.'

"After Adam and Eve were banished from the Garden, Eve asked, 'Adam, do you still love me?'

"Adam replied, 'Who else?'

"I come to you, today, with a topic that I have never preached or written on in nearly sixty (now seventy) years as a subject of the Eternal King. It is a subject that I find disheartening for it lays bare the enmity which the world of man has for the law of the Creator, God.

"Nonetheless, this is a subject which must be touched upon. May we do so with Christian love and respect as we endeavor to point out not our bias, but the Truth of the Scriptural model. It is sad that less than three-percent of the population has allowed their hatred of the Christian message to bring us to this point.

"I know that this sounds harsh. It is. That is wrong; it should not be so. A harsh message cannot be our message into the world. Our only true message is that Jesus Christ died in time so that others could live in eternity. As fallible men and women we will sometimes act out of frustration that our faith is so blatantly attacked.

"Again, this should not be so. It is a human reality. Although saved from our sin we are still products of humanity and will sometimes allow our hurt to fester into emotional bruises. Please do not allow the bruises caused by the blows of others to become unsightly blemished upon the face of our religious duty.

"For the record, and I do stand behind what I will say

here today, even as it shows a spiritual weakness in myself, I do not oppose the concept of same sex, i.e., homosexual marriage. It remains a sin against God, nonetheless. But, to be bluntly honest – it just ain't any business of mine unless I am asked to take part in such celebration. Most Christians, while agreeing that homosexual marriage is a sin, would have essentially the same feelings.

"So, why do we even mention the fact? There are answers to that question. One of them is pragmatic. We have to do so because the very foundation of our ability to be true to our faith is under sustained attack on this very front. While I will affirm that the marriage of two men, or of two women, is none of my affair, we are increasingly being forced, or at least attempted to be forced, to take a part in these marriages in various manners. This makes it our business. To hold true to our faith, a supposed right under the first amendment of the U.S. Constitution, is often denied under penalty of law.

"We are all familiar with the recent kerfuffle over a law in Indiana which was designed to protect the religious rights of Christians. Such diverse groups as the Christian Legal Society, the Southern Baptists, the National Association for Evangelicals, the American Civil Liberties Union, and the Citizens United for the Separation of Church and State were signed on as supporters of the law.

"This law did not need to be 'refined,' as the seemingly weak-willed Governor of Indiana seemed to argue; this law needed only to be enforced so that florists, bakeries, photographic studios, churches, pastors, and even pizzerias would be allowed their own freedom of religion. This law had nothing to do with bigotry except for the bigotry of those who would argue that their 'rights' were such as to force others to act in ways contrary with long established religious tradition.

"Such ought not to be allowed. This is no different than it was among the ancient Romans who brought the full force of some rather radical laws to bear against those who refused to account the emperor as 'divine' and to thus 'degrade' their allegiance to the Lord. Note that, in the main, these early Christians were not asked to give up their faith. They were only asked to subjugate their faith to Caesar.

"We have already had activist judges who have argued that we must 'accommodate' the 'law of the land' when there is conflict with our religious duty. A presidential candidate in 2016 argued that it will be necessary that our 'religious views' must change due to the 'new societal norms.'

"Folks, this is not the way of Christianity; we are to be a 'salt' that will season society, and a 'light' to lead the general society of man into a better life even on this earth. (Matthew 5:13-17)

"When the churches allow society to lead them, we find a weakened Christian message and eventually we lose sight of our specialness as a people of God. With Peter we need to give the sublime message of our Christian duty. 'Then Peter and the other apostles answered and said, We ought to obey God rather than men.' (Acts 5:29)

"Thus, do we ever need to argue if we are to be true to the Savior who willingly died as victim to unjust application of the civil and religious law in order that He might become The Sacrifice which cleanses our souls and purchases our salvation.

"What brought about this statement of Peter? To find the answer to this we need to back only two verses. In Acts 5:27 and 28 we find that the religious authorities have brought the disciples of Jesus before a court.

" 27 And when they had brought them, they set them before the council: and the high priest asked them, 28 Saying, Did not we straitly command you that ye should not teach in this name? and, behold, ye have filled Jerusalem with your doctrine, and intend to bring this man's blood upon us."

"We could answer, 'We have no *religious court* in this land so this is not an 'apples to apples' application. Well, what pray tell, is a court that has taken upon itself to argue how it is that we are to live our religious lives it is not a 'religious court?'

"Then, of course, there is the 'court' of public opinion which is fanned by the haters. I read an article in the local newspaper a few weeks ago. (Well, a few years as this is now being typed!) The title of the article was, 'How about a little hate with that Pizza?' No one, to my knowledge, has come forward to allege that the Pizzeria in question has ever refused service to anyone. No one! The only 'hate' I have seen in the entire episode was furnished not by the Pizzeria but by the haters with vitriolic speech and threats of violence. That includes the writer of the newspaper article.

"Again, the Pizzeria has refused service to no one. They have only expressed an intent not to take part in any 'same sex marriage' due to the owner's religious convictions. It seems more than passing strange that one person can cause an entire town to remove a Christmas display because they are offended. But one Pizzeria is not allowed to be *offended* by a demand that they go against their religious convictions.

"Who was it that decided that 'Christian convictions' are to be considered as 'Civil Crimes?'

"This is a 'First Amendment' issue. More importantly, this is an issue that is two-thousand years old – does the state have the right to tell Christians, who are harming no one, that they cannot enjoy freedom of religion in their beliefs? Proceed carefully here. Or, can someone claim that their 'rights' are more important than my relationship with the God of Creation?

"Tread carefully here because this is the issue.

"By the way, the answer to the above question as to 'who' made this choice, is judges who have overridden the will of the people. At the time of the original writing of this article, nearly all of the thirty-seven states which allowed same sex marriage had same sex marriage enforced by a panel, of judges; nearly all of these states had voted against the proposal in referendum at the ballot box. Judges then said, 'the sanctify of the individual ballot box? – maybe not!'

"Very few states have voted 'this is what we want.' Very few judges have told these states, 'tough, this is what you got.'

"O. K. There's been a lot of talk from me; that is not very important. Let's take a look at what is important: The inspired and preserved Words of God.

"Since this issue of same sex 'marriage' is often considered as a 'gay' issue, we should probably consider the etymological term of 'sodomite.'

"As an aside, I do reject the term 'gay' for homosexual because it is not a term which describes anything. It is a word imported without importance. One may be 'gay' without being homosexual as the word describes one who is generally happy with his present situation. The extreme anger and hatred shown both to and from the 'gay' activists suggest quite another reality.

"I am a Baptist. That word describes one who religiously is persuaded that one must be a believer baptized only by immersion. That is descriptive, the term was originally 'anabaptist' and referred to the propensity of the Baptist groups to demand that a convert be rebaptized when joining their ranks.

"But I digress.

"The word 'sodomite' was originally applied to the male temple prostitutes of heathen gods. These men and boys who were 'consecrated' to the acts which were of their worship. The female counterparts among their ranks were termed 'prostitutes.'

"Deuteronomy 23:17 forbids that any money gained through these immoral activities could ever be used in the furtherance of worship. This prohibition would apply both to the 'consecrated' female temple prostitutes and the 'free-lance' ventures as well. It would also apply to the temple sodomites, males, as well.

"Israel had no such history of temple prostitution. This prohibition was a reminder that such could not be tolerated within the nation. The broader lesson contained within the prohibition is that a sinful venture can in no way be used, or even, considered proper in a righteous light.

"The words 'sodomite' and 'prostitute,' although used to describe the concept of temple prostitutes were not limited to that use. It would be my guess that the town of Sodom was named due to the prevalence of such iniquity throughout the town. The reasoning is that the city gained a 'nick-name' due to the prevalence of the activity.

"Whether the name of the city, Sodom, came from that sin (I think it obvious that this is so.) or not, I think it obvious that the verb 'sodomite' stands, beyond even the consideration of irreligion – which I would also be led to believe was rampant within Sodom. The word 'sodomite' does not refer at this time to a person who resided in that city. In current use the word refers to a person who practices the sin for which that city was known.

"In the nineteenth chapter of Genesis we read the sad tale of Lot and his family. Scripture informs us that two angels came to warn Lot of the impending doom of the city in the fires of the judgments of God.

"Lot pled with these two angels, who appeared in the form of men, to spend the night in his home. Their expressed intention to spend the night in the streets of the city was met with more pleading from Lot for the men to stay in his home rather than in the street.

"As we read the narrative, we soon find the reason that Lot was loath to allow these men to sleep in the streets. A mob came to the home of Lot and demanded that these men (actually angels) be given to them so that they could have carnal relation with them. Lot was appalled at this request. He even offered the men his two virgin daughters instead. The mob refused this and demanded the 'men.'

"Modern revisionist commentaries will often list the sin in this place as forcible rape in an attempt to downplay the fact of homosexual acts. The fact that Lot did offer his daughters to this same mob would mitigate against that conclusion, although the idea of the forcible rape planned is certainly a sin. But, to ignore the fact that homosexual lusts were the root cause of the incident is to ignore the reality of the situation.

"In the Pentateuch, the first five Books of Moses, we

read of the establishment of the religious duties of men under the time of the Law. But this is an often-overlooked fact, we also read of the establishment of the civil government which would rule Israel. Another good thing to keep in mind is that the physical events of Old Testament are often used to illustrate spiritual truths which we need to consider even in the Age of Grace. We are not at liberty to worship God in any manner which we might claim.

"His Word has called us to worship in the manner which He has given to us. Both Cain and Able offered sacrificial gifts to God. (Genesis 4;1-10) While Able offered from the flock of his sheep, Cain offered from the fruits of his tillage. In Genesis 3:21, we read that God replaced the leaves with which Adam and Eve and clothed themselves with animal skins to cover their nakedness. This was, of course, a prophecy of the sacrificial death of Jesus for the sins of humanity. This was also an indication of proper worship.

"In Leviticus 20:13 we read: 'If a man also lie with mankind, as he lieth with a woman, both of them have committed an abomination: they shall surely be put to death; their blood shall be upon them.'

The displeasure of God toward homosexuality extends beyond the religious devotion of the heathen to encompass the daily walk of humanity.

"The fact that this is considered a capital crime is illustrative of the severity of the offense.

"As another aside: I once listened to a sermon which called this the worst sin possible. That is not true. Any sin can be forgiven when there is true repentance in a person's heart. The single worst sin which can be committed is to refuse to accept Jesus Christ as Savior. From this sin there is no court of appeal.

"Accept Him while you may for the time will come when you will stand before Him. Without this salvation experience there is no possible result but condemnation.

"For those who might argue that the above is 'Old Testament,' I would remind you that this is one Bible. The Old Testament truth is relevant in all times.

56

"Nonetheless I do want to consider one New Testament passage in relation to the sin of homosexuality. I will only quote Romans 1:26-28. I invite you to read the entire passage in its context. The truth is not diminished.

' [26] For this cause God gave them up unto vile affections: for even their woman did change the natural use into that which is against nature; [28] And likewise also the men, leaving the natural use of the woman, burned in their lust one toward another; men with men working that which is unseemly, and receiving in themselves that recompence of their error which was meet. [28] And even as they did not like to retain God in their knowledge, God gave them over to a reprobate mind, to do those things which are not convenient.'

"Once again, the fact of sin is that it is sin. It is a violation of the order which God created.

"I have had discussions with a former pastor about the homosexual situation. He disallowed that there was a 'gay gene.' He said that such was not possible because it was a 'gene' which would have long since have been 'bred out' of humanity which would negate the possibility of it being introduced into another generation.

"I disagreed. I think that there may actually be such a 'gene' as to produce a propensity toward homosexualism. I would argue this because of the sin nature which is present within all humans born of man and woman. This type of condition shows one who stands is desperate need of the 'new birth' which is available only because Jesus Christ died in time so that we might live in eternity.

"I have actually had people argue with me that homosexuality is a 'natural' thing because it is often found in animals in the wild. If it is 'natural,' it is because sin has infected the natural order of the present world. Romans 8:22 gives this insight: 'For we know that the whole creation groaneth and travaileth in pain together until now.'

"This is because of sin!

"In Second Peter 3:10 we read that the present earth will be judged with fire. The first judgment upon the earth

57

was with water which only covered the sin of the world. The final judgment upon this earth will be of fire which will destroy the incumbent sin within the physical world. God will reestablish this world perfect with no trace of either sin or tempter to sully the goodness of His creation. Those transported to this 'new heavens and new earth' will live in true peace and true harmony as they worship the Creator, God.

"We have looked briefly at the seriousness of the sin of sodomy. It is an evil which God will not bless.

"This is not to deny the reality of 'common grace.' God has promised to give a certain common grace to His creation. In Matthew 5:45 Jesus notes that the rain falls on the just and the unjust. But there is no spiritual grace available for the person who has not accepted Jesus Christ as his own Savior. Even to the Christian there can be no grace levied on the account of sinful, willfully sinful, activity. There will be chastisement.

"Now, finally, we turn our attention to the concept of marriage. It has been said that God created Adam and Eve, not Adam and Steve. Although a flippant phrase, this is nonetheless true. In Genesis 1:27-28 God said

' 27 So God created man in his own image, in the image of God created He him; male and female created He them. 28 And God blessed them. And God said unto them, Be fruitful, and multiply and replenish the earth, and subdue it: and have dominion over the fish of the sea, and over the fowl of the air, and over every living thing that moveth upon the earth.'

"I am not going to get into a long discussion of 'God created man is his own image...' Let me just note that this has nothing to do with our appearance. God is Spirit; we are physical. When God breathed the 'breath of life' into the nostrils of Adam (Genesis 2:7), He gave to the race of humanity an eternity of existence. Each one of us will either spend an eternity of bliss in fellowship with our Savior, or we will spend an eternity of regret outside His presence. This is the reality of our human existence.

"You may have noticed that in the passage from

Genesis, God gave the command that man and woman would 'be fruitful and multiply.' This simple fact requires an Adam and Eve rather than an Adam and Steve. This is not to argue that each couple will have children. It is to argue that to make an attempt to thwart this course is to exhibit a refusal of the obvious leading of God. Some will be past child bearing age when married. There will be other problems which prohibit the pregnancy of the woman. We do find Biblical examples of this.

"At the 'Tower of Babel' the sin was not in the building of the tower. The sin was the purpose of the building. The command of God for those people was that they overspread the earth. The purpose of the tower was to hold them together in one location. God said, 'go;' they said, 'no!' Therein was the very base of their sin.

"This same construct is at the heart of the sin of homosexuality. It is a perversion of the purpose which God had established in the original creation of humanity.

"Such a perversion of God's intent is sin against the holiness of God and any such union would not gain either His favor of license. The traditional marriage is sanctified by God is shown by the fact that Paul spoke of the union of man and woman as an 'honorable estate.' (Hebrews 13:4)

"It must be acknowledged that early marriage did not follow the same customs as we find in our day. I remember when I proposed to my wife. I was on a three-day pass from the military while Linda was on a three-day weekend from her employment.

"This was not the way of earlier marriages or of many marriages even in this day in parts of the world. These marriages were often brokered by the parents of each of the parties involved. The man and woman may have even been small children at the time. It was not even necessary that the bride and groom had even met. The parents brokered the wedding.

"The family of the groom gave an agreed upon price to the family of the bride to secure the betrothal. In the case of Jacob in the Old Testament account, this price was seven years of labor – *twice!*

"We see in this an illustration of the worth of a Christian. Paul said, 'For ye are bought with a price: therefore glorify God in your body, and in your spirit, which are God's. ... Ye are bought with a price; be not ye the servants of men.' (First Corinthians 6:20 and 7:23)

"For all intents and purposes, the betrothal was the beginning of the marriage. It was the legal beginning of the marriage. The betrothal was not the time when the couple began to live together as man and wife; that might come about a year later as the groom prepared a place to which to bring his bride. From the betrothal forward, however, the two were considered as the spouse of one another.

"The betrothal ceremony was certified by witnesses who agreed that the terms of the marriage were contracted and accepted by both families.

"The bride then returned to the home of her father to await the day when the marriage would be consummated. This would be a time when there would be a bridal procession and a marriage supper which would be held in the home, generally speaking, of the groom's parents. These 'marriage suppers' could take up to two weeks to conclude.

"After the marriage supper had concluded the marriage would be consummated by the entrance of the groom into the bridal chamber to be physically joined to his wife.

"The bridal procession is still seen in today's weddings. The concept hearkens back to another type of wedding 'ceremony' wherein the bride was captured during battle and simply escorted back to the home of her new husband. There was no betrothal in such a case.

"It should be mentioned that there was no betrothal in the case of a concubine. There was no dowry, and often no one to whom it might have been paid. We read of Sarah (Genesis 16:2) giving her maid to her husband as a concubine. This indicated that a man could not take a slave to be a concubine without the consent of his lawful wife.

"The essence of the marriage was the removal of the

bride from the home of her father and into the home of the groom, or the home of his family. There may have been a reading of the terms of the marriage (betrothal) contract; this would have been the extent of the 'marriage ceremony.'

"It is to be expected that the fact of marriage would be touched upon in the Pentateuch. In these five books were given the laws governing the setting up of the nation of Israel as a people. We must also reference in regard to this that such statutory law was also considered religious law in the theocratic nation of Israel. Therefore, under the Scripture we must find that marriage, while a civil matter, is a matter governed by religious precept and law. This is an often-overlooked fact.

"Scriptural marriage is forbidden with close relatives among these early Hebrews. The only exception is the Levirate Marriage whereby the widow of a man who died childless would marry either his brother, or another 'close kinsman,' as in the Book of Ruth, to raise up a child which would be considered as the offspring of the deceased.

"Beyond this, there were three grades of prohibition in marriages among these ancient Hebrew people.

"First, there could be no intermarriage with the Canaanites.

"Second, the males could not marry either the Ammonites or the Moabites,

"And, Third, the males could marry the Edomite and Egyptian women.

"We must also note that the offspring of such marriages above were not allowed full access into the religious life of Israel.

"In the patriarchal age, wherein the men were the absolute rulers of the home, it is interesting to note that there are three rights given to the women. There was the right to food, clothing and conjugal consideration. (Exodus 21:10) These may seem small rights but the very fact that these were legal rights was a step beyond that given to women of many in the surrounding cultures.

"Outside of the Pentateuch there is little Biblical reference to marriage. Jesus and the apostles did speak ethically and theologically about marriage when the subject arose. An example of this is the discourse concerning divorce which Jesus viewed as a modification occasioned only by the permissive will of God.

"We must note that there is little evidence of polygamy among the Jews of the time of the sojourn of Jesus upon this earth.

"Genesis 4:19 records the first plural marriage by Lamech. We see Deuteronomy 17:17 giving warning against such. The 'infighting' of the wives of Jacob gives us another warning against the practice. Passages such at Psalm 128 and Proverbs 31 seem to ascribe marital happiness and contentment to monogamy concerning a husband and a wife. The story of Solomon stands as another warning against multiple wives.

"Marriage is spiritually important. The institution typifies the relationship between God and His people. (Old Testament examples: Isaiah 54:5; Jeremiah 3:1-14; Hosea 2:9,20. New Testament examples: Ephesians 5:25-27; Revelation 19:7-9) Marriage is often used as an allegory of the relationship (faithful and exclusive) between God and His people.

"It is important to note that God has placed the man as 'head of the home.' (Genesis 2:18; 3:16; First Corinthians 11:8-9; Ephesians 5:23-33; Colossians 3:18-19; First Peter 3:1-7) If the passage from Ephesians is read, we will find that this headship is to be in the spirit of Christ to his church. The primary function of the husband is to love his wife rather than the '*lord it over*' her.

"The concept of a same-sex 'marriage' disallows the clear teaching of God concerning even the relationship within marriage. We are all familiar with the number '6-6-6-.' Whenever we hear this, we say, 'Oh, the number of Satan.' It isn't. six is the number of a man. Three is the number of the Trinity of the Godhead. What we actually see in the number is a picture of man trying to make himself God.

"This, of course, cannot be. He will come up short every time.

"We must also note that seven is the number of the perfections of God. No matter how often it is repeated, the six of man will never equal the seven of God.

"This same general construct is shown in the anti-Biblical concept of same-sex 'marriage.' Christians who hold to Biblical teachings are branded as 'haters' because they choose to obey God rather than sinful mankind. As to taking part in a homosexual 'ceremony,' God has given us clear instruction in Ephesians 5:11. 'And have no fellowship with the unfruitful works of darkness, but rather reprove them.' We cannot take part in these affairs. Our choice is simple, as was the choice of first-century Christians – we can choose to obey God, or we can choose to obey man. Where will you stand?

"I have done a little survey on the subject of homosexual marriage from the Scripture. Not surprisingly the Scripture is somewhat silent on the matter. The silence, broken in a few places, is an elegant statement that homosexual unions are not in the plan of God.

"The word 'husband' is mentioned 102 times in Scripture. In 97 of these times the reference is in relation to a male. Three times there is no specific reference although the intimation is male. Twice the reference is to God. I found no reference to a male and male consideration.

"The word 'wife' is mentioned 374 times in Scripture. 371 of these mentions concerns a reference to a female. Three times there is no specific reference. I found no reference to a female and female consideration.

"The word 'marriage' is mentioned 17 times in Scripture. Four of these times there is reference to man and a woman. Twelve times only the man is referenced. One time only the woman is referenced. I found no reference to either a man and a man, or a woman and a woman relationship.

"The words 'lay with' and 'lie with' occurred 29 times. Twenty-six of those times there is reference to male and female. This would include both lawful and unlawful considerations. Once there is a reference to male and male; this is in Leviticus 20:13. 'If a man lie with mankind, as he lieth with a woman, both of them have committed an abomination: they shall surely be put to death; their blood shall be upon them.' I found no cases of 'lay with' or 'lie with' concerning woman and woman.

"I found two references to bestiality. 1) Leviticus 20:15 – 'And if a man lie with a beast, he shall surely be put to death: and ye shall slay the beast.'

"2) Leviticus 20:16 – 'And if a woman approach unto any beast, and lie down thereto, thou shalt kill the woman, and the beast: they shall surely be put to death: their blood shall be upon them.'

"I would only further note that in regard to this bestiality that one time refers to a man and one time refers to a woman. Both cases are covered.

"Many years ago, I watched a man make a demonstration with a 'milking stool' which contained three legs. He made the point that three legs on the stool will support him during the task of milking a cow. To lose any of these legs will make the milking stool unstable and unfit for its assigned task.

"It is said that there are three pillars of modern civilization: marriage, private property, and the state. It is a projection of the state's power into the other two pillars which has upset the 'milking stool' of civilization which we witness daily in the newspapers, and often in the streets.

"There are three great human events in each life: Birth, marriage and death. All three contain serious theological and religious importance. The birth of a human life concerns a soul coming into this world with the need of eternal salvation.

"Marriage concerns us not only as a consideration of birth but also as an allegorical picture of the relationship between the individual and God. Distort that relationship and the physical picture of the grace of God is distorted.

The individual born into such a society will not, humanly speaking, see the reality of his need for salvation.

"Death concerns the disposition of the soul. May our actions in regard to the other two events never be used as a wedge used to drive anyone into Christless eternity.

"Above all, we must be true to our Lord Who died in time so that sinners such as I could live in eternity.

"It is the state which gives us the legal freedom to stand on the Word of God. When that ability to stand is withdrawn the milk will be spilled even before the milking stool has fallen. It is those great events of life which are made understandable only by the stands of religion. Remove the right of religion to do her work, and to stand her ground under God, and the life of a man, or woman, is meaningless and devoid of spiritual direction."

While I do believe that I have included sufficient Biblical evidence to cite the concept of same-sex, homosexual, marriage as sin in that it does violate the standards which God has set down in His inspired and preserved Word, the Christian must still not judge those caught in the snare of this sin. We can cite the obvious, that this is not the will of God for humanity. What we cannot do is be harsh toward the sinner. It is a sin against God, not a sin against us – unless we are compelled to take part in some way.

The only time this would be a sin against us would be when we are expected to take part in the ceremony of the celebration. At that point we are being asked to sin against the clear teaching of Scripture. We cannot join the sinner in his sin. (Second Corinthians 6:17; First Timothy 5:22 – "Lay hands suddenly on no man, neither partake of the other men's sins. Keep thyself pure"; Second John verse 11.) The point is that when we take part in what we know is wrong, or we encourage one to take part in what the Bible has informed us is wrong, we are siding with Satan against the Person of God. This, it should be obvious, is sin against God on our part.

You may notice that First Timothy 5:22 was quoted while the other verses which enjoined us not to partake of sinful actions simply because someone would want that we do so, were only listed by their *Scriptural address.* I did this because the verse in Second John is very relevant to me.

Many years ago, maybe around 1980, I received a phone call from what I consider to be a cultic religious organization asking me to take part with them in a community outreach. When I declined, the caller asked me "why?" My answer from my theological understanding was, "Because I worship the God of Heaven and Creation. You worship demons from hell." I am tempted to put this response down to religious zeal, and youth. That would be wrong. Simply put, I was stupid! It is possible to disagree without being boorish and rude.

Do you think that I'll ever be able to talk to one of the practitioners of that religions about the love of God, or anything about the saving grace of Christ? We could easily reference John 3:16 in reference to my stupid answer. John 3:16 starts with the phrase, *"For God so loved the world..."* As Christians, our first and most important task in this life is to call others to saving faith in the God "Who so loved the world." I am a proud fundamentalist. May we hold to the fundamentals of the faith as we seek to spread that faith of eternal salvation out into the world. Generally speaking, we cannot expect to win for Christ those we have attacked! We must never depart from out Scriptural views. Be we often need to depart from our pride and combative attitude.

It is easy to see that, with the incident of the woman taken in *the very act of adultery*, that Jesus did not attack the woman for her sin. He even acknowledged her sin when He said to *"go and sin no more."* But these Pharisee's were very zealous for the Scripture. They were the strictest sect of the day. They wanted to stone her, as the Scripture demanded. John records that, upon being ask to sentence this woman to death, Jesus stooped down and began to write in the dust. We are not told what Jesus wrote.

We are only told that the accusers of this woman left one by one as He wrote.

My guess, again it is only a guess, is that Jesus wrote the words of Leviticus 20:10 on the ground. This may have been the verse being used to demand the death of this woman. Leviticus 20:10 says,

> *"And the man that committeth adultery with another man's wife even he that committed adultery with his neighbour's wife, the adulterer and the adulteress shall surely be put to death."*

 The woman's accusers had conveniently left one of the parties out of the equation.

Where was the man? The woman would not be committing adultery by herself. Whether she was married or not is irrelevant in this case. The woman had been set up to take a long fall by these paragons of religious righteousness. My guess, again it is only a guess, is that one of their own number had tempted her to commit the sin in question. The hard fact is that they had misapplied the Scripture to teach evil rather than to consider the purpose of the reference. Jesus did not disregard the Scripture. He upheld it and saved the woman's life, physical and eternal.

Read the Scripture. Jesus is never seen as attacking people. He is always seen as polite even as He was committed to the righteousness of the Law and Scripture. The only instance of His ire showing through has to do in reference to the religious people who would have kept Him from the sinner.

My answer to the phone call was not only wrong, it was not a true Christian response as it in no way honored Jesus. And, it could easily be seen that it could have kept others from finding true faith in the true Jesus.

TRANSGENERATIONAL ACTIVITY

The next point I need to consider is an issue on which I am not well informed. I will admit that I am not trained in the biological things of humanity. I would hesitate to touch the subject except that I am a student of Scripture and can understand that which is against the Scripture of God's will for His human creature. The concept of what is called "transgenerational" activity is something which has touched my extended family twice. Their activity in this area will not change my love for them. It just won't. This does not mean that I would condone their activity. It just means that I do not have the right to condemn them for it. However, I am fully cognizant of the fact that God does judge them as breakers of His moral law.

Nonetheless, there is no way that I can consider this as a sin against me. The only offended party would be the God of Creation.

I have not been affected by their actions. But I must acknowledge that their actions have been a violation of the purpose of God's creation of humanity. That is a definition of sin. What was the sin of Adam and Eve? Was it not that they disregarded God's will by partaking of the *forbidden fruit?* The act of taking the fruit of a tree was not sin. But, the act of taking part of the fruit of *that* tree was a violation of the expressed will of God. That was sin.

Sin has eternal consequence. It separates from God. It aligns one with Satan. That eternal soul, which was bestowed by the very breath of God upon Adam was an establishment of an eternity of the existence of that soul which was created to have a close relationship with the Creator, God.

CHAPTER 5

THE PERFECTION OF THE ENVIRONMENT AND SPIRIT

The entrance of sin into this spirit of Adam meant that he could no longer enjoy that fellowship with the Creator. However, that fellowship was part of the perfection of the environment into which the creature was introduced. Since that fellowship was broken by sin, it could no longer be fulfilled in the coming eons of eternity. What must also be considered is that Adam, as the first of the human kind in this creation, would pass on his new, and sinful nature, on to all of his offspring. We, today, are also part of the offspring of Adam. The situation of humanity is expressed in the third chapter of Paul's letter to the Romans, verse 23,

> *"For all have sinned and come short of the glory of God."*

This fact means that all who have not had their sins forgiven are not eligible to spend and eternity of fellowship with the Lord. Still, there is that eternal spirit which must abide for all of eternity. Since these spirits tainted with sin cannot abide for eternity in the fellowship of the Lord, they will abide with the one they have served as sinners in this world. Speaking of the judgment which follows the Great Tribulation Era and the setting up of the Millennial Kingdom of our Lord, Jesus spoke these words in Matthew 25:1,

> *"Then shall he say also unto them on the left hand, Depart from me, ye cursed, into everlasting fire, prepared for the devil and his angels."*

This is a consignment of all unsaved persons to an eternal home in the eternal judgment of God's wrath upon Satan and those who are his followers.

Since the situation I've been "talking around" for the past few sentences has to do with the fact of transgenderism. The question must be asked, do I have a Biblical rational for branding transgenderism as a sin? After all, there is not a single sentence in all the Scripture which mentions transgenderism. Is there any reason to consider this as a sin?

Since there is no Biblical evidence to brand this as "sin," does this lack of evidence disallow my stating of this as sin? It is not surprising that there is no Biblical evidence concerning the word "transgender." But neither is there any mention of tobacco smoking in the Scripture. But we are on solid ground when we condemn the practice. There are verses which tell us that the believer's body is the "temple of God." (Romans 14:7-9; First Corinthians 3:16; 6:9; 15-16; 19; Ephesians 2:21-22; First Peter 2:5) We all now understand that smoking tobacco can harm the body of the believer – actually anyone. This, in effect, will harm the temple of the living God. The Holy Spirit of God lives within the life of the believer in Jesus Christ as Savior. This use of tobacco is thus seen as sin. This is also a principle which is relevant to the issue of transgenderism.

Still, I would like to look at this situation from another standpoint. Let's consider this situation from the perspective of God' creative actions. I'm going to examine the creation of Adam, and of Eve, in the chronological order of the Scriptural record.

Before I begin, I would like to explain one thing in reference to the chronological record. Many have looked at the creation being explained in the first chapter of Genesis and then restated in the second chapter. These have often imagined that there was more than one writer in Genesis. This is not necessarily the fact of the matter. Hebrew poetry must be considered in cases such as this. Hebrew poetry is not based on repeated rhyming words being used. Neither is Hebrew poetry exactly as we might employ *free verse*. Hebrew poetry will use a *thesis line* and follow this with a restatement, generally providing an expanded consideration of that thesis. I will attempt to illustrate this with an appeal to the

Psalm:1:1:

> *"Blessed is the man that walketh not in the counsel of the ungodly."*

How is a man to be blessed; he will not walk in the wisdom (counsel) of the person who is ungodly. The verse (Psalm 1:1), then continues,

> *"nor standeth in the way of sinners."*

We see the progression continue,

> *"nor sitteth in the seat of the scornful."*

The blessed man will neither congregate with (stand) or have close fellowship with ("sitteth in the seat of the scornful") the sinners.

Now we can consider the creation of man from Genesis 1:26-27.

> *V.26 "And God said, Let us make man in our image, after our likeness: and let them have dominion over the fish of the sea, and over the fowl of the air, and over the cattle, and over all the earth, and over every creeping thing that creepeth upon the earth." V.27 "So God created man in his own image, in the image of God created he him; male and female created he them."*

Notice that God said, *"Let us."* It has been argued that this speaks a plurality of majesty of God. This, of course is not wrong. But there is little purpose in God suggesting His majesty in this manner so soon after the creative acts have displayed His majesty and power. It has also been suggested that this speaks of God addressing the angels. This view would not be correct since the angels are, themselves, created beings who have no creative power. The truth of the matter is that this is an early reference to the Trinity.

Another thing to be noted from this first cited verse is that God has set man as the overseer of His creation. This would give rise to the destructive effects of the sin of man over all the terrestrial creation. Consider this fact in relation to Romans 8:22-23 –

> *" 22 For we know that the whole creation groaneth and travaileth in pain together until now. 23 And not only they, but ourselves also, which have the firstfruits of the Spirit, even we ourselves groan within ourselves, waiting for the adoption, to wit, the redemption of our body."*

Simply stated, sin does not occur in a vacuum. Even our own sin has consequence beyond our understanding.

Back to verse 27 of that first chapter of Genesis. We were created in the image of God. This cannot be in reference to our appearance. God is spirit while we are of the temporal creation. The meaning here is that we have a *creative* bent within ourselves, along with the eternity of existence as given by the breath of God. This writing is a form of creation, not of nothing as was the creation of the universe. Considering my writing talent, this could probably be a creation *into nothing*. This is a form of the creating of fashioning. God is said to create Eve. While this is true, the Bible clearly show that the creation of Eve was by fashioning her from the rib of Adam.

We also have the ability to plan and reason within us as the result of this breath of God. While many of the animal kingdom will reason out a path to stalk and find their food, or to evade their predator's, only man has the ability to plan in an abstract manner. We can, for instance, plan to write a book and distribute it for sale. While this may contain an element of "food procurement," it is only by an abstract thought process that this plan may be considered.

We could also consider the last word in that 27th verse. The use of "them" speaks of separate persons among humanity.

Now, in the second chapter of Genesis. We find the creation of Adam.

> *"And the LORD God formed man of the dust of the ground, and breathed into his nostrils the breath of*

life; and man became a living soul." (Genesis 2:7)

Up until this point the creative action of God had been pleased to make these animals, physical features such as water, and so on, from nothing. Now, with the creation of Adam, God *fashioned* him from the elements of that creation. The creation had been made so as to provide a habitat for the human race. Now, Adam is formed from the elements which had been put in place to sustain Adam.

This would suggest that, while being created to have fellowship with his Creator, Adam was also to care for that environment which had been provided by God. We ought not shirk our duty to God by refusing our duty to the planet as a God-given residence.

Discounting the concept of the spiritual (foolish to do so!) we see only three levels of life in our created experience. The first of these would include the plant life which consists only of body. I would include the one-celled entities such as bacteria in this classification. These have no real reasoning ability and only respond to events in relation to their created status. Flowers are not conscious of any need to face the sun, for instance; they only do this because this is part of their created *make-up* to do so. Viruses, such as the Covid 19 strain, do not plan to kill humans; it is only their pre-programed *feeding and replication manner* which cause such to happen. This is so, even when this means that they will remove the means of such feeding and replication. For this reason, I would consider that they have been *re-programed* by the sin of Adam which has infected all of the temporal creation. (See comments on Romans 7:22, above.)

The second of these *levels of life* would consider the animal kingdom. This time we must consider the concept of soul. The soul is that which energizes the body to act. Lions, for instance, are not simply killers. But, killing is how they obtain their food. They will hunt, and plan strategies to efficiently kill. The same concept would apply to the cow who finds a way to gain their food from the very grass of the field. We may argue that they only feed thus because it is their nature. But this rational will not fully explain why these who eat fresh, green, and moist grass will also eat dried out hay if that is all that is available. True, hay is simply a form of dried grass. But hay is still not the same as grass. The lion in a cage at a zoo, or in the wild if he is able to find it available, will eat food which he has not killed. He knows what nourishment is needed for his life to be sustained. The fact of hunger might lead him to this decision. The same general argument could be continued throughout the animal kingdom.

The third level of life would concern the above verse, Genesis 2:7. While we may argue that Adam was already comprised of a soul, this would argue that he was the same as the brute beast of the field. Ah, but the *entire phrase* records that the breath of God transformed Adam into *a living soul.* This was an immense change in Adam. God had placed the reality of *spirit.* As such. Adam was now of *tri-partite* nature. He was now possessed of an eternal nature which would never go out of existence. He was now the possessor of body, soul *and* spirit

We now need to revisit Genesis 2:17:

> *"But of the tree of the knowledge of good and evil, thou shalt not eat of it: for in the day that thou eatest thereof thou shalt surely die."*

This phase does not concern the *spiritual death* of Adam. Consider what Paul wrote in I Corinthians 15:44:

> *"It is sown a natural body; it is raised a spiritual body. There is a natural body, and there is a spiritual body."*

This is speaking of the Christian who has died a physical death before the Rapture, he will be raised to a spiritual existence.

Consider this tree, which became the object of sin in the hands of the human who chose to disobey the law of God, was actually a method of pious worship had the humans put aside their desires and rebellion and simply obeyed the Words and Leading of their

74

Creator. Consider that sin is simply a refusal to obey and follow the dictates of the Creator, God.

This would be a good place to consider another verse from Genesis.

> *"And God blessed them, and God said unto them, Be fruitful, and multiply, and replenish the earth, and subdue it: and have dominion over the fish of the sea, and over the fowl of the air, and over every living thing that moveth upon the earth.* (Genesis 1:28)

Reading this verse, one can only agree with the Rabbinic tradition which notes that God created humanity as a sexual being. Sex, properly applied, is to be considered as a blessing from God. We cheapen that blessing when we consider sex as a tawdry element.

Another verse to consider is Genesis 2:18:

> *"And the LORD God said, It is not good that the man should be alone; I will make him an help meet for him."*

Please notice the loving care of God in relation to the coming sin of man. God's plan was to give the human race all that would give joy and contentment to Adam and his race of humanity.

PERFECTION OF HUMAN EXPERIENCE

There is only one more verse that I would add to this perfection of human experience. Hebrews 13:4:

> *"Marriage is honourable in all, and the bed undefiled: but whoremongers and adulterers God will judge."*

I don't think we need to explain the word "adulterers," but the word "whoremonger" is not as familiar to our ears. This word is listed as number 4205 in Strong's. It is described as "...from pernemi (to sell; akin to the base of 4097); a (male) prostitute (as venal), i.e. (by analogy) a debauchee (libertine):--fornicator, whoremonger." The obvious meaning is that sex between individuals with a marriage vow between them is to be considered as a blessing. Any other consideration is not sanctioned as the blessing of God.

Contemplate that all of the plant life was given for food; but one species of plant life was prohibited. We may consider the words of Paul as concern's those "Who [have] changed the truth of God into a lie, and worshipped and served the creature more than the Creator, who is blessed for ever. Amen. (Romans 1:25)" You will notice that there is a class, as referenced by the Apostle Paul, who have the evident truth before them and have denied that truth and treated it as false. Instead of accepting this truth, they side-step it and seek other, seemingly to their own minds, eternal truth which they mistakenly find within the temporal world of creation.

The final passage to be studied in this section is from Genesis 1:21-24:

> [21] "And the LORD God caused a deep sleep to fall upon Adam, and he slept: and he took one of his ribs, and closed up the flesh instead thereof [22] And the rib, which the LORD God had taken from man, made he a woman, and brought her unto the man. [23] And Adam said, This is now bone of my bones, and flesh of my flesh: she shall be called Woman, because she was taken out of Man. [24] Therefore shall a man leave his father and his mother, and shall cleave unto his wife: and they shall be one flesh."

Here we see the fashioning of Eve. I suppose that it would be possible to claim that Adam, in some sense of the word, gave birth to Eve since she was drawn from his body. That analogy doesn't really compute because Eve did not gestate with Adam. God caused a sleep to come upon Adam and operated by removing a rib, and then closing up the incision.

With this rib from Adam, God fashioned the person of Eve. She was a distinct person, separate from Adam. Still, Even shared much with Adam. We see the plan of God in that life always rises from life. There is no hint of any evolutionary process here. Adam passed on his general physical and spiritual attributes to Eve. She was born with the *breath of God* incumbent within her life. She was a person with an eternity of existence. She also felt an affinity toward the Lord, her Creator, as did Adam. And this predisposition to worship the Lord was part of the make-up of Eve.

In the 23rd verse we find Adam admitting his own nearness to the person of Eve, even while making note of her being another separate person. The passage closes with a prophecy from Adam arguing the special union of the man with his spouse.

Through all of the above we find that God created the man, and the woman, to be each of a special creation. They are acknowledged to be, at the point of creation, to be who they are. There is the male – Adam, and there is the female – Eve. There is no suggestion that either of them ever could, or ever would, be anything other than that which they were created to be.

Then something horrible happens in the third chapter of Genesis.

AT THIS POINT SIN ENTERS

Both Eve, and Adam, take part of the *forbidden fruit*. At this point sin enters into the creation of God's perfection. Sin is a horrible cancer within the creation. It is that which causes the will to sin. The will to sin is simply for one to place their own will above the will of God. It is to disagree with God as to the fundamental soundness of His creative words. As such, this causes a deep rift to open between mankind and God. Mankind, the creature is drawn into an opposition toward God. There is no longer any real area of agreement with the goodness of God. This causes a separation between man and God. Gone is the prospect of an eternity of existence for the human with the Divine. Rather than finding a home in Heaven for all eternity, mankind finds that his eternal mode of existence for his eternal spirit is not with The Lord in Heaven, but with the accuser of mankind, the devil, in the eternal Lake of Fine of the *Second Death*. Sin has made this the reality of those who have refused God and followed the way of sin as given by Satan.

As we postulated about the possibility of a *gay gene* causing some to struggle with homosexuality, so, too, there may be a *transgender gene*. The same answer would be for both aberrations to the plan of God for humanity would be at play in both. This would be curse of sin causing harm to the lives of some of the creation of God.

There are several mentions of the potter's wheel in Isaiah and Jeremiah that speak to those who would argue the "God made me like this!" The most salient quotation for our present discussion would be found in Isaiah 29:16:

> *"Surely your turning of things upside down shall be esteemed as the potter's clay: for shall the work say of him that made it, He made me not? or shall the thing framed say of him that framed it, He had no understanding?"*

Those born as XY remain XY. Those born as XX remain XX.

To misquote *Popeye the sailor man,* they am what they am. This is further proven by the fact that their "medications" to facilitate the "transition" must be maintained or the body will try to go back to what it is. They remain to be what they were, and still are in their basic structure.

TO HOLD TO RACISM IS TO FAULT GOD

In essence, I would find the same reasoning as I would for racism. To hold to racism, or to transgenderism, is to fault God for making not only a mistake, but a willfully wicked mistake in creating the variants among humankind, we *all* after all, are of the same race – the human race. "And hath made of one blood all nations of men for to dwell on all the face of the earth, and hath determined the times before appointed, and the bounds of their habitation" (Acts 17:26)

As an aside, I must note that there was a certain so-called fundamentalist school several years ago who used this verse to deny *foreign* students the right to date while attending their college because their habitation was not the same as some other students' native habitation had been. But the habitation spoken of in this verse is the earth. The word "dwell" earlier in the verse is the same word used for habitation. Note that the dwelling place is described as *"all the face of the earth."* That word is number 2733 in Strong's "katoikia, residence (properly, the condition; but by implication, the abode itself):--habitation."

The conclusion reached in this short study is that it is a sin for one to call God either mistaken or malicious in His creation. While acknowledging that I have offended some, I have the duty as a theologian of the inspired and preserved Word of God, to stand correct according to those God-breathed Words. They are always Yea and Verily. This is so even when we, as some of my readers will conclude, do not wholly agree with that Holy writ.

I do not see the above, either same sex marriage or transgenderism as the greatest sins of our nation. They are, nonetheless, sins as described by the Word of God. Neither, although this is also a prevalent sin in our society, is racism the greatest sin.

To view racism in the nation, I would take you back to 1840 to view events that transpired in northern Illinois. The story of Sukey Richardson, and her four children standing on the steps of a county court-house where Abraham Lincoln had often tried cases, being sold back into slavery from which they had only recently escaped, is told in Dark Angel by Martin Litvin. (Black Angel, Litvin, Martin, Log City Books, Galesburg, Illinois, 1972) Mrs. Richardson was not her real name. It was assumed from the slave master who had obliged Sukey to bear four of his children. She felt that she had earned the right to the name of her master.

Although only the eldest daughter of "Mrs. Richardson" was sold back into slavery at that time, she was soon to be bereaved of all of her other children by that former slave master and father of her children. Make no mistake, the fact that they were, biologically his children. that slave master did not afford them any rest from the rigors of their condition of servitude. They were still simply part of his stock of property to be sold, if he wished. Or, whatever else he wished. His property, his right. That was the law of the land.

At this point I would copy a short section concerning "The Black Laws" well, some of them. Please consider that Illinois was considered as a "free State" at the time. This is excerpted from Mr. Litvin's book as referenced above.

"EXCERPTED FROM THE REVISED STATUTES OF ILLINOIS approved March 3, 1845 - The following is in chapter 54 under the head of 'Negroes and Mulattoes':

"Section 8, Any person who shall hereafter bring into this State any black or mulatto person, in order to free him or her from slavery, or shall directly or indirectly bring into this State, or aid or assist any person in bringing any such black or mulatto person to settle and reside therein, shall be fined one hundred dollars on conviction and indictment, before any justice of the peace in the county where such offense shall be committed.

"Section 9, If any slave or servant shall be found at a distance of ten miles from the tenement of his or her master, or person with whom he or she lives, without a pass or some letter or token whereby it may appear that he or she is proceeding by authority from his or her master, employer or overseer, it shall and may be lawful for any person to apprehend and carry him or her before a justice of the peace, to be by his order punished with stripes, not exceeding thirty-five. At his discretion.

"Section 10, If any slave or servant shall presume to come and be upon the plantation or at the dwelling of any person whatsoever, without leave from his or her owner, not being sent upon lawful business, it shall be lawful for the owner of such plantation or dwelling house to give or order such slave or servant ten lashes on his or her bare back.

> "Section 12, If any person or persons shall permit or suffer any slave or slaves, servant or servants of color, to the number of three or more, to assemble in his, her or their outhouse, yard or shed for the purpose of dancing or reveling, either by night or by day, the person or persons so offending shall forfeit and pay the sum if twenty dollars with cost to any person or persons who will sue for and recover the same by action of debt or indictment, in any court of record proper to try the same.

> "Section 13, It shall be the duty of all coroners, sheriffs, judges and justices of the peace, who shall see or know of, or be informed of any such assemblage of slaves or servants, immediately to commit such slaves or servants to the jail of the county, and on view or proof thereof to order each and every such slave or servant to be whipped not exceeding thirty-nine stripes on his or her bare back."

There were *"good"* slave masters who provided a form of "share cropping" for some of their slaves. Most provided decent medical care and food. Most did not, it was even illegal in many cases – if not most – to provide even basic education. Housing, of course, was made available; this was in the form of "shacks" of low value and comfort.

The concept of medical care, while mostly out of the reach of the poorly paid northern factory worker, was not an act of benevolence. It was simply, when offered, a matter of taking care of a valuable member of the "owner's" herd of stock.

Even considering what might be considered as a minimum standard of living for the slave, there was always the prospect of slave families being broken up by the sale of some of the family to distant ports by "slave auctions." This was not infrequently done as a manner of raising cash for the plantation expenses. Not only did the plantations raise "cash crops," they also raised the "stock" of slave persons for sale to the highest bidder.

Also, as in ancient Rome, any sort of discipline, up to and including the maiming or killing of a slave, was not considered as a matter for law enforcement. It was simply the right of the *owner* of his *breeding stock.* Many of the "owners" did consider the slaves to be "breeding stock" as they were quick to sell them to the highest bidder to make a few coins. The splitting up of a family was not considered out of the ordinary. It was just not, really, considered any more than we might sell off, or give away, a litter of kittens or puppies.

There have been studies which argue that the standard of living for the average northern factory worker was lower than that of the southern slave; these may not have considered all of the available information. While the northern factory worker was paid a substandard wage, and was subject to losing his employment on the whim of his employer. After all he could be easily replaced by the next man in the street. He was not likely to see his spouse or children sold to another factory without any sort of recourse. Still, neither have those who can find no improvement in race relations examined fully all of the evidence. It has been over seventy years since President Truman desegregated the U. S. armed forces, proving that white people can, and do, serve competently under whatever race they may perform that service. Within a few years of President Truman's action, the schools were also desegrated. This should have produced an equality of educational opportunity. Social segregation has somewhat stymied this effect.

We should also reference the voting rights acts of the 1960's. These should have had more effect on public policy than they have had. Sadly, too many have become simply part of various *voting blocs* rather than agents of change and modification. These "voting blocs" tend not to study the policies of the various candidates as they lazily follow the *party lines* with their votes. This tendency lowers the need for the party they favor to look for the needs of this group because they will follow habit rather than need. Meanwhile the other party tends to ignore these groups since they know that they have no chance of gaining their vote. Poor voter action will produce poor public policy actions.

CHAPTER 6

ONE MORE PUBLIC SIN: ABORTION

There is one more public sin I would like to comment on. First, let me access the words of Moses as he led the people of Israel toward entrance into the promised land.

> *"And thou shalt not let any of thy seed pass through the fire to Molech, neither shalt thou profane the name of thy God: I am the LORD."*
> (Leviticus 18:21)

Moses was generally very anxious that the Israelites would not follow the false religions of the people of the land. His warning was that this would draw the people away from the LORD. Molech was one of these heathen gods. Passing their children through the fire was a reference to human sacrifice to this god. Moses argued that their children should not be killed in this manner. This is a recurring theme throughout the Pentateuch and other Books of Scripture. (cf: Deuteronomy 18:10; Second Kings 16:3; 17:17; 21:6; 23:10; Second Chronicles 33:16; Psalms 106:37-38; Jeremiah 32:36; Ezekiel 16:21; 20:26; 20:31; 23:37)

It is interesting that we are currently looking with horror on the morality statistics of this current pandemic. We are told that over 500,000 have died from this disease. Our entire culture of free travel and free association has been changed in light of these numbers. But we care little that this number pales in comparison to the number of deaths each year from abortion. Abortion is touted as a near-sacred rite among many. Our culture of death in this regard has lowered our cultural ability in respect to the sanctity of life. This is a sad reality which is a picture of one of our most prevalent national sins. It is an affront to God, who created life and humanity.

By the way, this makes the pandemic only the third highest killer of the day: Both heart disease and cancer kill more. So does abortion; but we are not allowed, under the political correctness doctrine of the day, to mention abortion as a killer. It is!

God had something to say about this mindset. One of the false religions, the worship of Molech, occurred at the time of Israel inheriting the land. This was one of the sins which caused the people of Canaan to lose possession of that land. They were a wicked people – especially in light of their treatment of innocent children. Are we any different? Several states have already passed laws allowing the killing of children who have survived abortion. This is known as killing of children through infanticide, although we will hesitate to call it such. The truth does, however, remain the truth.

THE KILLING OF CHILDREN

God pronounced opposition to the killing of children by offering them to the false god Molech by burning them to death. This sounds grisly to our refined ears. Is it any grislier than the dismemberment of children through certain types of abortion?

We have mentioned a few of our national sins. I find one sin that is often not considered as sin. But, any reading of the minor prophets would argue that this may be the greatest national sin. So, what is the greatest sin in our nation today? The biggest sin, the soul damning sin, is to refuse to accept Jesus Christ as one's savior.

However, shortly behind this sin there is one that we can historically chart as the beginning of our slide into most of the other national sins – at least the added prevalence of these sins in the past 50, or so, years. In order to properly begin a discussion of this great sin, it might be good to consider the words of Moses from Deuteronomy 12:11.

> *"then there shall be a place which Jehovah your God will choose to cause his name to dwell there; thither shall ye bring all that I command you: your burnt-offerings, and your sacrifices, your tithes, and the heave-offering of your hand, and all your choice vows which ye shall vow to Jehovah."* (First

Kings 11:36; 16;2; 26:2; Second Kings 21:4;
Second Chronicles 6:5-6; 7:11; Daniel 9:18)

This place is identified as Jerusalem. It was where the great temple of Solomon was located. These are the words of Solomon, set down in the inspired and preserved Words of Scripture, as he dedicated that great temple to God.

> *"If thy people go out to battle against their enemy, whithersoever thou shalt send them, and shall pray unto the LORD toward the city which thou hast chosen, and toward the house that I have built for thy name"* (I Kings 8:44)

CHAPTER 7
THE GREAT SIN OF JEROBOAM: IDOLATRY

Next, we must consider the great sin of Jeroboam. Jeroboam led ten of the twelve tribes to rebel against the Davidic line which God had establish to rule over His people from the city of Jerusalem. These *breakaway* tribes founded the kingdom of Israel – the Northern Kingdom of Israel, while the descendants of David continued to rule the Southern Kingdom of Judah.

Jeroboam had a political and religious problem. God had set His temple in the city of Jerusalem. This city was within the bounds of the kingdom of Judah. Certain sacrifices and ceremonies were required to take place within Jerusalem. Read First Kings 12:26-28 and see how Jeroboam decided to solve his problem.

> *"26 And Jeroboam said in his heart, Now shall the kingdom return to the house of David: 27 If this people go up to do sacrifice in the house of the LORD at Jerusalem, then shall the heart of this people turn again unto their lord, even unto Rehoboam king of Judah, and they shall kill me, and go again to Rehoboam king of Judah. 28 Whereupon the king took counsel, and made two calves of gold, and said unto them, It is too much for you to go up to Jerusalem: behold thy gods, O Israel, which brought thee up out of the land of Egypt."*

Notice what Jeroboam did. He instituted a form of idol worship and he reinterpreted the very religious history of Jacob's people with a lie which would keep the people from their duty toward their God. As we read the history of the kings of the kingdom of Israel, we find that each of them sinned in this manner. They followed the sin of Jeroboam. Each of the kings of the kingdom of Israel keep the idolatry of the *calf-gods* of Jeroboam and the false view of the history of the people.

May we take a look at Second Kings 10:31, as an example of this false religious institution:

> *"But Jehu took no heed to walk in the law of the LORD God of Israel with all his heart: for he departed not from the sins of Jeroboam, which made Israel to sin."*

Notice that even as the kingdom of Israel was led away from God by their kings, God still claimed them as His Own people. No! God has not cast away His people. There is yet to be a glorious future for the people of our Savior's national, historical family when He renews them with the miracle of the New Covenant.

More on that in another study. For now, however, let us look at what Isaiah had to say about the situation in the religious life of the people of his time.

> *"In transgressing and lying against the LORD, and departing away from our God, speaking oppression and revolt, conceiving and uttering from the heart words of falsehood."* (Isaiah 59:13)

While not departing to calf-gods, in the manner of the kingdom of Israel, Isaiah made notice that the people of the kingdom of Judah had also departed from the pure words of God into a false set of religious values and practices.

THE KING JAMES BIBLE

We have departed from the pure Words of God as we have jettisoned the reliance of our churches upon the King James Bible. It's not the King James Bible which is, itself, important. It is that upon which the KJB was founded. We have removed ourselves from that upon which the KJB was based. We have removed ourselves from **the Traditional Text** in our rush to embrace the newer *versions* of the Critical Text.

Most will not argue that well over 90% of the available ancient Biblical manuscripts are of the Traditional Text type. Less than 5% of the available evidence comes from the non-traditional text manuscripts. In point of fact, we cannot really argue for a preserved Scripture if we use **the Critical Text**. No edition of the CT ever saw the light of day before 1881 and the work of Westcott and Hort. But Bible colleges, and those who wish to appear wise and *in line* with current thought, will champion the new text.

We will even find references in the center columns of our King James Bible's which say that *"the oldest and best texts"* argue against the words of the true Bible of history. We now have so many Bibles that we have no Bible. It is possible, and has been done by some, to *fact check* many *Scriptures* to find one that will align with our own pet doctrinal stances. I have read books, by men I do admire and respect, that list eight or ten different *bibles* in their bibliographies, and of course add, *used by permission* after the many names of the versions used.

God has given His true Bible to be used by His directive. We need not ask the permission of man to use His Words.

Has anyone noticed the lack of influence of the Christian religion upon the culture of the day since we abandoned the use of His Words as given into our language by The Bible which is proudly based on His inspired and preserved text? Could it be that our lack of spiritual power is in direct correlation to our lack of trust in His Words?

The golden calves of our new Bibles are also a change in our history. Before this time the general consensus of Fundamentalism was that the fact of inspiration was based on a Verbal/Plenary understanding. Realizing that we cannot claim such with the new critical text, fundamentalists and others have begun to champion a new concept of "Concept Inspiration." The words, we are told, were never preserved. We only have the general concept as an inspiration of the Biblical story. I would like to introduce another of my own works, prepared for the 2016 Dean Burgon Bible Conference, on the subject of "The False Construct of Concept Inspiration."

CHAPTER 8

THE FALSE CONTRUCT OF CONCEPT INSPIRATION

"And changed the glory of the uncorruptible God into an image made like to corruptible man, and to birds, and fourfooted beasts, and creeping things. (Romans 1:23)

"May we never divorce our words from the Words which God has inspired and preserved for His children.

"I come before this body one more than that I had expected to do. Both of us ought to be somewhat saddened by that eventuality! Here I am again doing my best to drive you to prayer. 'Lord, how long is he going to talk!'

"I do hope to reach my usual level of competence. Happily, I have set the bar so low in the past that this should not be a problem.

"I have intended to drive to this year's DBS meeting. What was it the poet say about 'time and tide?' As far as 'tide' is concerned, if I were found lying on a beach someone would call 'Green Peace' to try and roll be back into the ocean. As for 'time,' I drive a 2003 Buick LeSabre. I was afraid that I might cause a gasoline shortage before I got all the way here! Besides that, I would have needed at least three weeks to travel, considering probable repair time!

"The real reason is that I just can't stand all the blaring horns. That noise is very distracting and it seems that nearly everyone else uses their horn at least three times in every mile. I don't understand it.

"I am a very careful driver at my advanced age. I drive at the speed limit of 45 miles per hour. Sometimes, when I feel adventurous, I will push it all the way up to 50.

"I am also a very polite driver. I have studied the situation and have found that nearly everyone drives in the right lane. So, I politely drive in the left land. Knowing that most of the exit ramps are off the right lane, I try to remember to keep my turn signal turned on so that I won't forget when I need to turn.

"Also, I nearly never used by cell phone when driving. I only use when I need to talk with someone. I never text at any time on that phone. That is partly because I would have no idea how to text. My grandson told me to add that information.

"This has been an example of the outcome of Concept Inspiration. I have said things that seem obvious to me at this age. Those things, obvious to me, might not actually be rooted in the reality of the situation.

"Another example actually did happen to me. I was visiting a lady from church who was in a nursing home. I hadn't taken my cane so I was a little tired after the visit. Somehow, I missed the door leading to the parking lot. I went up to a nurse and asked, 'How do I get out of here? I can't find the door.'

"She offered to help; she took me by the arm and led me to the Alzheimer's ward! Like any adherent of Concept Inspiration, she had heard what I had said and processed the information according to her preconceived notion of what it should mean.

"Concept Inspiration does not always concern itself with spiritual truth because the basic idea is to convey the translator's idea of what might have been said rather than what was actually said. By necessity the translator must do this from his frame of reference in the created world of physicality and time.

"Unfortunately, for this translator's work, God has sent us words of physicality and time to explain the eternal and spiritual. The translator's focus is so fixated on his audience, which resides in the created world, that he may overlook the fact that God had intended His audience to see and understand the things of eternity and the spiritual.

"Before I get into my talk today, I'd like to mention a few words. Tea party. Constitution. Freedom of Assembly. Right of free speech. Freedom of Religion. That's probably enough.

"Now that we have the friendly people from the deep federal government and IRS listening in, we may begin. I would suggest something to you guys from the Federal Government who are listening in. I would remind you all that there is a God Who actually does control the times and the seasons of the world's governments. We leave our fates completely in His hands.

"Don't worry about it. Any day now the Lord will appear in the clouds and take His Own to be with him. At that time, you and your ultimate master will be given free reign for a few years.

"In the meantime, we have more important things to do than to even consider you. We have the work of the True Master of the Universe to proclaim into the world. True Christians would never consider doing you harm. The true Christians would never be doing any sort of harm toward those who are 'infidels' toward our religion. That just is not what God expects of us. We pray, and God acts. Our earnest prayer is that you would accept the free grace of Jesus Christ and accept Him as your own Savior.

"Now, as to the issue at hand. The idea of concept inspiration is simply to give a paraphrase of what the paraphrasers believe true Scripture to be. Well, now that this is done, I guess I can stop.

"I know that I got your hopes up when I said that. But I can't stop yet; I have a few minutes left to fill.

"Here comes the filler!

"The first thing I want to note is that Concept Inspiration is a slippery slope to Doctrinal Error.

"Believe me, I know what error is. I played baseball when I was younger. As far as catching the ball in Right Field, the coach kept trying explain the difference between volleyball and baseball.

"Note that the idea is what the paraphraser believes is the sum of his conception for inspiration. Sadly, as he works from the 'false Scripture,' - that of the Critical Text, even his concepts are flawed.

"This all seems so harsh. Unfortunately, it is also so very true.

THE JUDGMENT OF GOD UPON AMERICA

"As in all paraphrase, the issue is not what the Writer has said but what the reader has read. The sum is what the reader is able to take from that writing as a message. Therein is the problem.

"The construct is not a '*Reader's Digest*' book review. The picture of concept inspiration is not of condensation but of believing that only the general message has been retained and not the words. In sum, God is only allowed to have said what the translator believes He has said.

"The problem is that is you take out the words you are likely to misapply the message. There are only eight notes in the musical scale. I know that with 'sharps' and 'flats,' and the loop of more notes above and below, that there are more. I don't really understand or read music. To be true, I couldn't tell a doe from a buck as to the notes.

"But, potentially all of the notes are encased in those eight notes from 'The Sound of Music.' Remove those notes and Mr. Beethoven would have been a farmer. Remove the Words from the Scripture and we have... Well, we simply have feelings and aspirations. We can never know what feeling mean or to where the aspirations might lead.

"'Concept' is a flawed concept even if it isn't repeated twice in the same sentence.

"In his wonderful book, 'The Complete Idiot's Guide to Jewish History and Culture,' Rabbi Benjamin Blech wrote concerning the Roman destruction of the Temple, 'It took four years from start to finish, but eventually, the (war) was over (in 70 C.E.) And when the Jews looked at their calendars, they recoiled with horror at the realization that the Temple went up in flames on the ninth day of Av ... exactly the same day, on which the first Temple had been destroyed,

"'What did this amazing coincidence mean? Clearly it proved that it was no coincidence! God must have been behind those two great tragedies.' Rabbi Blech continues with the words of Rabbi Abraham Isaac Kook, former chief rabbi of Israel: 'The Temple was destroyed only because of the needless, undeserved hatred between Jews. It will only be rebuilt because of needless undeserved love – when Jews show their concern for others, even when they differ from them in their values, ideas, and levels of observance.'

"As strange as it may seem, I – a Calvinist, Biblicist, Dispensationalist, Baptist - agree wholeheartedly with the Rabbi in that conclusion. That agreement is conditioned on my view of God's great prophecies concerning the time of Jacob's trouble. (Jeremiah 30:7) which we understand as the end-times tribulation.

"Do you think that the learned Rabbi would agree with me in all of my conclusions? I don't either! But, why not? Are we not both speaking from same understanding of the time of Messiah? I see Messiah as turning the hearts of all Israel to true religion during this time of testing.

"Contributing to our disagreement is the fact that I see Messiah as Jesus. Messiah has already come. He is coming back to this world again to 'make good' on the promises given to Abraham's descendants. He is coming back to end the 'the times of the Gentiles' and restore the sovereignty of the Throne of David on this earth. I would imagine that the Rabbi sees the words of the New Testament as a fantasy of a Gentile world system which has appropriated, and greatly changed, the great truths which reside in the Jewish Scriptures.

"We in this room understand that the Old Testament Scripture and the New Testament Scripture must stand together as they were written by the same God. Our focus in the concept of these prophecies in the Jewish Scriptures, the Old Testament, is colored by our belief system. And, obviously, the leading of the Spirit.

"Concept Inspiration seeks to divorce the need for the words to fully support the concept. It is not interested in the actual words. It is only focused upon the general message as understood by the learned theologian. That theologian, meanwhile, will view the 'general message' only through the glasses of his own theological system of exegesis. In this we might see the danger of concept inspiration as a prescription for the easy entrance of false doctrine tied to a possible false view of Scripture

"How could this be? An Armenian theologian might fall down a set of stairs and break his leg. This causes him to miss an important series of meetings. His inattention caused him to not give needed instruction to others. He worries that his inattention on the stairs has caused him to fail the Lord.

"A Calvinist theologian might fall down the same set of stairs. I am going to assume that he broke his 'other' leg. It just would not seem right for the champion of 'free will' and the adherent of 'election' to both break the same leg!

"It is the Calvinist's firm and reasoned belief that it was the Lord Who caused him to fall. That particular fall had been decreed in eternity, past. It was the Lord who caused him to fail to give needed instruction to others. His worry is understanding why God did this to him and what it must mean to his future as a spokesman for the Lord.

"Words have real meaning. They just do not have the same meaning to all. Whether you live by a 'creek' or a 'crick' is dependent upon where you live!

"Several years ago, my daughter was going to be baptized in a small lake near the town in which I lived. I had been to the lake many years before, but I did a 'google search' to refresh my mind as to how to get to the lake.

"My journey began on an interstate highway. Then I turned off onto a 'hard road.' The 'hard road' became a gravel road. The gravel road became a 'two rut' dirt road. That ended in a corn field with no lake in sight. It seemed that Google had did an oops!

"A farmer in whose drive I had to turn around, said, 'As near as I figure it, Google must have shot a satellite image when I had taken down a few rows of corn and mistaken that for a road. But you can't get there from here.'

"Apparently I had not been the only 'outsider' to attempt to find the lake by google search. I probably should have used a good road map from the state!

"Along this same vein, some very intelligent scholars and spiritual *leaders* have decided that they know enough about the eternal and spiritual that they can understand the 'general concept' of Scripture in these areas. I am certain that they are correct, just consider how much power and influence the church has into the world of man since those scholars have begun to exalt their own knowledge while abandoning the King James Bible as produced from the Traditional Text and begun to trust the new Critical Text. Who needs the leading of the of the actual Words which God has placed in His Scripture?

"Well, unless I want to end up in a 'spiritual cornfield' which keeps me from finding the Lake of the Living Water, I guess I do!

"Did you ever try to put together a new toy for your grandkids without reading the instructions. If the 'toy' is a new computer, you had better get those grandchildren to help! They live in a 'computer world.' They understand the beasts of binary blustering!

"Although I did not try to consult with Mr. Spock on this, I do find it illogical to believe that any man of physicality and time would understand the reality of eternity and spirit well enough to reconstitute a lost Scripture without being able to use those words which God gave to explain the land of 'hereafter' to the people of 'here.'

"Those who do the best at this exercise are probably those who were brought up with a reliance upon the KJB until some college professor taught them that they did not really need the words which God had originally inspired. To borrow from Proverbs, 'Pride goeth before destruction, and an haughty spirit before a fall.' (Proverbs 16:18)

"Eternity and the spiritual are a strange county to our human ears and eye. We can hear nothing, we can see nothing, of that land. It is all conjecture. Just look as some of the fanciful attempts of so many to explain the concept of an 'afterlife.' We must have the real Words of the real God, given in His miracle Book to understand the truth of the eternal and the spiritual.

"Jesus told Nikodemus, 'If I have told you of earthly things, and ye believe not, how shall ye believe, if I tell you of heavenly things?' (John 3:12) In the very next verse Jesus explained to those of us whose entire life experience is on the earth. 'And no man hath ascended up to heaven, but the he that came down from heaven, even the Son of man which is in heaven.' (John 3:13)

"By the way, if you simply follow the words in that sentence, you must agree that Jesus is God. He speaks of Himself as being on both earth and in Heaven at the same instant!

"One who considers only the concept, not the words, of the Scriptural message is like trying to find a specific lake without a map. He might well end up in a cornfield.

"I remember back in the misty olden days when I took my test to get my first driver's license. I had to bring my own horse and buggy! One portion of the test had a series of shapes. 'These are the shapes of the different signs.' I was told, 'Your job is to tell us what should be written on each of the signs.'

"How did I know? 'Show me the real sign and the message will be written on it.' That was my plea.

"If one does not know what is written on the sign, how can he understand what the sign is pointing toward? If the Words are discarded from the preserved and inspired Scripture, how can we understand what is the Message?

"Well, if it is from the Critical Text, I do not believe that it is possible to call it *a preserved Scripture*. As such, neither is it an inspired Scripture.

"If my grandson asks me to go outside and play 'catch' with him. I have understood the general message. If I go outside with a football and he has brought his baseball glove, we have not each gotten the specific message. Those words are important signposts to explain the real meaning of the message. Remove the Words and the message can be anything one might wish it to be!

"This is true even when that person is wrong!'

"Concept Inspiration has been described as a slippery

slope to Doctrinal Error. I would now consider that Concept Inspiration is a slippery slope to Demented Exegesis.

"Oh, look. The fat guy is using an alliterated outline. I wonder if he has three points. Yep, I do. When my father built the house I grew up in – I grew out much later. But that is another story. Anyway, he built the house with a new gas furnace. He also put in coal chute.

"Many years later I ask him why he had built it that way. His answer? 'That's the way my father taught me to build a house. So, that is the way I build a house!'

"So. Three alliterated points? That is the way I was taught and that the way I do it. The only problem is that I do it so poorly!

"That same 'that's the way I was taught' is also the reason that so many have departed from the Traditional Text. Someone has taught them his fallacy; in order to be true to some professor – or some college, they *fall in line* rather than studying the issue with prayer for the leading of God. 'Follow God? I need to be true to a professor or a college.'

"Demented exegesis?' Back to the Rabbi's book one more time. 'The trees, it is said, came before God to complain about the ways of creation. 'Why,' they asked, 'did you create us and at the very same time allow the creation of an axe that would be used to chop us down and destroy us?'

"You foolish trees,' answered God. 'Have you never noticed that the axe has a wooden handle? If you had not first given of yourselves to the enemy, it would be incapable of ever doing you any harm!'

"Just as an aside: Have you noticed that I have accessed the same book, which has no relevance to the issue at hand, in my talk? Why? Because I have recently read the book and it is a very interesting book. The reading has allowed it to become a natural part of my thought process to the extent that I will relate certain stories from the book to use as arguments in favor of my thesis.

"We need to read our Bible's a little more often. It is a very good Book. It contains some very interesting things within its covers. A serious perusal of the Bible will allow its precepts to become part of our thought processes to the point that they will just 'crop up' in our general conversations. Reading the inspired and preserved Scripture is a very good witnessing tool!

"And, the reading of Scripture will also cause us to be more attuned to the work of the Holy Spirit within our lives. Not a bad bonus!

"And now back to our regularly sponsored convention.

"Folks, if you want to understand the lack of power in the churches of this nation, go back to the construct of Concept Inspiration. From this mindset, or possibly vice-versa, came the reversal of the local churches use of the verbal/plenary understanding of Scripture.

"I say 'possibly vice-versa' in recognition that those who placed unholy hands on the Holy Words of God's inspired and preserved Scripture had to find an excuse for their actions in explaining away their 'operation' upon the verity of Scripture with the diagnosis that they were only, in their opinion, operating on a corpse.

"What better way to destroy the faith of the people in the pew, and to enhance one's own prestige and power than for a *'Bible College'* to explain that the Words are no longer 'in the house.' Only those with special knowledge could rightly understand the message of God. No need to bother the Spirit. The experts can take care of you much as did the medieval clerics of the Church who prohibited the Bible even being printed in the language of the people.

"And, you foolish people thought that Gnosticism had died out centuries before! Why did you think that we were being fed a diet of Gnostic texts for our Spiritual food? Satan understands that we cannot be defeated when stand in the Spirit. Well, we are told that we no longer have a need, or a trust for the guidance of the Spirit or the Words of God. After all we can't really trust either, can we? Better check with the human experts of theology. Them we can trust. Them we must trust. Our real Bibles have been taken from us!

"You had better believe that we can trust the Lord and His inspired and preserved text which underlies those Bibles – no matter what man may say! That is why these meetings are taking place. It is a very short view to say that we simply stand for the underlying text of the King James Bible. Folks, we stand against Satan and all of his nefarious wiles. We can never do that without the power of the Spirit and the Words of the inspired and preserved Scripture.

"When I went to war, I was issued a gas mask, a 'flak jacket' and a rifle. It would have been foolish to just invite the enemy over to talk with us. 'We will learn your language and play some records of your favorite songs.' This would not have been advantageous to our efforts. I suppose that we could have called it a 'Contemporary War,' and offered a 'Traditional War' at a later time. Isn't that what we are doing with our churches in this day?

"Where did our power go as a 'church' in this day. It didn't go anywhere. We have just learned not to trust that God-given power; we've learned not to trust it. Instead, we have become very friendly with the enemy of our souls.

"Why are Christians not 'up in arms' into the world of those who disagree with us and demean our Savior? I don't mean that we should hate; that is anathema to our Christian message of the love of God. We just need to boldly proclaim the message of the evangel.

"There is a new law in the land. It is called 'hate crime.' You readers of George Orwell might remember it by the term "wrong think;" it is – at its base – a crime of thought rather than action. Most crimes are not committed by those who love those they harm. We are to engage in an attitude of Love. There really is a Heaven to gain and a Hell to shun. The most hateful thing we can do to others is to allow them to go into a Christless eternity without ever being given the opportunity to hear the message of the Cross.

"We do need to preach this message sweetly and compassionately. But, bottom line, we do need to

101

preach it into the world of lost humanity. Spice the witness with prayer that God would convict souls and approach those souls with grace and honest love.

"I have heard that a man named McVey blew up a building several years ago. Another man, actually several, attacked a couple of abortion clinics. Another man... Well, we pretty well ran out of examples of 'Christian hate.'

"I would appreciate it if someone could give me examples of these people seeking to win the lost to Christ. Where is the evidence that the much-maligned *Christian right* engaging souls with the message of the love of God and the need for accepting Him as Savior? The Great Commission calls us to win the lost for the Lord. Although we are called to be a 'salt of seasoning' into the world at large; we are not called to change society except as we call the lost to salvation.

"In the Gospel movie 'A Distant Thunder,' one young lady turns in her friends for being Christian during the Tribulation Era. I can't quote exactly, but she saw some of her friends facing the guillotine. The friends were shocked. They said that they thought she was a Christian.

"Oh, silly,' she says, 'Anyone can say that they are a Christian.'

"There was a group from a church (so called) in, I believe, Kansas a few years ago. They would come to funerals of service members to protest. They came to the town where I lived twice. Although they were busy protesting, they never – at least to my knowledge, ever give out so much as one gospel tract. They saw themselves in the guise of the Old Testament prophets. To my understanding of true Christianity, they had no witness of the religion of Christ. I could not call them 'Christian,' although the media certainly did.

"Read the Book of James. Were any of the 'Christian Terrorist' as mentioned in the newspapers actually Christian? Show me the fruits of the Spirit in their lives. I can find no reason to call them 'Christian.' The only purpose in calling these types of groups 'Christian' is to paint the true Christian with the broad brush of intolerance. Now, there is an obvious hate crime.

"Folks, when we see the national media, late night comics and other religions seeking to 'lay the axe to the root' of our tree of Christianity, just remember that our boorishness is often supplying the wood for the handle of that axe.

"We have done this by inviting world's music into our 'praise' of the Lord. We have done this by inviting the world to pass judgment upon our Scripture. If they don't want to read it, we don't want to use it. Can't we trust the Spirit of God to empower His Own Words of witness? We have done this by inviting the culture of the world into our church services. We have done this by bringing a polite speech, which foregoes speaking of the gospel message, to our pulpits by not warning of sin and Hell.

"Run references for me to the verse where Jesus said, 'All of you are fine. We are just like you and you are just like us. Come on over and join us. You have nothing to lose or fear. I offer religion without commitment, piety without pain and Heaven while remaining earthly.'

"Then we offer a baptism of immersion into the cesspool of Satan's world and culture. Sad. False. Popular!

"In the interest of spreading the pure Gospel of Jesus Christ, some have even been known to offer a *'Lord's Supper'* of beer and pretzels. What version did that come from. I am certain that it came from no version which had anything to do with the real Words of real Scripture.

"And our new ~~Gnostic~~ groveling to the demands of the world's religious leadership applauds our efforts to 'Win the Lost without the Cross!'

"This all began with the laying down of the Sword of the Spirit and accepting the *sweet leadership* of the world of Satan's lie. The Words of God remain perfect and powerful. The Spirit remains to witness of the Way of God into the world. Even the following is useful to humanity. Within the pure Words of God we are able to see our imperfections vividly contrasted with the Perfection which IS God.

103

"To any reasonable person this is reason enough to fall to our knees and accept the free Grace God has offered to each of us.

"Sadly, but truthfully, Concept Inspiration is a slippery slope to Downgrading the Eternal One. It cannot work, of course. But the finite minds of the people of this world always seek to enlarge themselves into something of importance in the world.

"Foolish people. They will never understand that this world is only a short way-station on the road to eternity. That reality is constantly ignored by those whose hearts and minds are darkened by the wiles of Satan and the words of his willing tools in the land of human intelligence.

"A major problem with Concept Inspiration is that it does tend to exalt the knowledge of man even as it seeks to give a 'modern' understanding of the ancient Scriptures. The consequence of this mindset is that the message of God is lost in the cross-cultural attempt to make the 'old' words of God reach the 'new' man of this present age.

"Solomon was a very wise man. I know that he sinned in the manner of his many wives. As I will quote from Ecclesiastes, I must also consider that this is a book of the wisdom of man displayed on the canvas of God's inspired and preserved Word. This is a true statement as concerns humanity. 'The thing that hath been, it is that which shall be; and that which is done is that which shall be done: and there is no new thing under the sun.' (Ecclesiastes 1:9)

"Now, I do understand that many things have changed since the time of Solomon. He never had to put gas in his chariot so he could travel around his kingdom. He didn't even have to plug his chariot into any outlet to charge it up. He did have to feed his 'chargers' oats so they could continue the trip.

"But Solomon was not talking about inventions. His subject matter was the essential nature of man. Man has not changed in the 3,000 or so, years since the time of Solomon. Man was created with the desire to worship. When he cannot find, more properly when he

104

refuses to accept the True God of creation to worship, he will find something else which his worship will be focused.

"To be honest, man is always willing to find something, anything, to worship rather than to direct his worship toward the God Who created man. This is so until the time when the Spirit sends conviction upon the heart of a man!

"By the way, we are to witness that need to the population of the world. We are also to pray, by name whenever possible, for the Spirit to send this conviction upon a man's heart.

"With Solomon, I would assume that part of his worship was centered upon women - but there was an important 'more!' Wealth and prestige must have also figured into Solomon's 'man-ology' in his personality.

"I would also assume that Solomon came back to the God of his father at some point late in his life. Isn't that the gist of Proverbs 22:6? 'Train up a child in the way he should go: and when he is old, he will not depart from it.'

"God is often so gracious as to allow us to often see our children and grandchildren reach out to him. But, I've often seen old people, some even as old as me!, come back to the God of their youth. They attribute this to prayers of their parents, grandparents, aunts and uncles, from years before. We may not see the fruits of our prayers and training on the world of woe but, even after we've gone, God still remembers to honor the prayer of faith.

"The point is that we have no need to 'update' the eternal Words of the Eternal God. God knew about everything that had happened, and would happen, long before our own heartaches may have begun. He spoke His Words from that eternal perspective which will touch the souls of men and women of any age. Even an age to come on this earth.

"We do a profound disservice to God when we argue that His Words were so buried within the created world that they lost their power sometime during some hippie celebration in 1968.

"Do the learned theologians of the day not realize that God is wiser and more powerful than all of them? God has no 'letters' after His Name for there is nothing that speaks more power, prestige and purpose than the Name of God.

"This mania to exalt man has led to the proponents of Concept Inspiration to depart from the obvious will of God. This extends to worship. Paul made an interesting plea in Colossians 3:16. 'let the word of Christ dwell in you richly in all wisdom; teaching and admonishing one another in psalms and hymns and spiritual song, singing with grace in your hearts to the Lord.'

"Did you notice that? Paul speaks of singing spiritual songs with grace in our hearts. If the singer can simply substitute the Name of Jesus with the name of 'Jessie,' and then take this same song to any tavern and sing it to the patrons, is that a 'spiritual song?

"Would the melody of the 'spiritual song' simply substitute a few pious words and be unrecognizable from the same song used in any tavern and sing it on a 'top 40' radio station?

"Watch the performers at those 'praise services.' Look at the vacant look on the faces. Look at their gyrations on the stage. Is this any different than that which could be found in any music hall of the world?

"But, we are told that we need to do this to reach the people of this day. Do we? To what are we calling them? From what are we calling them?

"As for the performers, and the 'Mosh Pit' that formerly served as a church sanctuary, swing, sway and swoon, they are in a very precarious position whether they understand it or not. They will attest that they are 'in the spirit.'

"They may well be 'in a spirit as they move into a state of submission to the sensual drives of the music and the numbing words which claim their spirituality; they have opened themselves to the spirit of this age. That is the beat. That is the content. That is the situation in which they may soon find themselves. They do not understand, under the soul numbing effect of their

106

ecstasy of the moment, that they are prime candidates for spiritual oppression.

"Some of the words may well have some claim on true spirituality. Everything else also claims a spirituality of the world of Satan's influence.

"Beyond this, these people would have no real defense. Jesus gave us the example of using Scripture to combat the temptations of Satan in the fourth chapter of Matthew. With the construct of Concept Inspiration removing the word from the message, these people are spiritually defenseless.

"The culture, entertainment, hopes, aspiration, everything about the Christian should be different from the world. We cannot exalt the pure God of eternity by wallowing in the culture of the impure god of this present world system.

"What has been done is to belittle the message of God and the God of that message. We have told Him that His Words can no longer reach the crowd of this age. We claim a need to join the Philistines so we can fight for Israel!

"We said earlier that humanity is of the natural creation of physicality and time. We can never understand the things of spirit and eternity without finding a guide book to teach us of the truths of that land.

"I have spoken much about the cultural results of bibles (small case intended) which are based in the construct of Concept Inspiration. That is because these new bible's, which have removed Words of God from consideration, have left only the temporal words of mortal man. Even the concepts drawn from this may not be considerations of anything God may have intended to relay to the spirit of His children on this earth.

"It is to be expected that this concept, and the bible's culled from its rational, will convey the culture of the spirit of the age rather than the Spirit of God.

"I remember the first college I attended after my high school graduation. It was a 'Bible College,' and proudly so. We were even given handouts explaining why we were superior to the other mere 'colleges' of the secular world.

"Well, now they are a university. They proudly proclaim that this is a great advancement for the institution. Back then they would have called it a large step backwards, spiritually.

"Ah; I digress.

"One of the first professors I sat under made the statement that Communism is a superior system for many people. What would the book I accessed earlier have to say about that? Isaac Jacob Rabinowitz, a renowned Talmudic scholar said, 'Marxism is contrary to Torah, which protects private property.'

"The point is that if a teacher in a Baptist Bible College could not even understand the concepts of this earth, how can we expect that scholar to lead us once the Words of Scripture have been plowed under by the cultivator of human intellect.

"Folks, it is quite easy to explain inspiration: It is plenary. That means that complete and perfect. It is verbal. That means that every single word and letter, even to the parts of the letters according to Jesus (Matthew 5:18), is perfect and eternal. It is the Breath of God. It is the Words of God committed to us down to this day because it is the eternal Word of God.

"Just the concept is not enough.

"That Concept Inspiration may give an incomplete, or as interpreted through the eyes of a theological scholar, a false view of that which God said. (I used the present form, rather than the past, in that previous sentence. The real Words of God are eternally new and true.

"I remember one time Ronald Reagan was running for president. He was doing poorly in the polls. His advisors realized that they were guilty of micro-managing his campaign. They decided to just 'let Reagan be Reagan.' He won in a landslide.

"Folks, look around you. We live in a day when the great revivals of the past are simply fond memory. We do not see the power of the Spirit evidenced in most of the churches of the land. We are trying every little trick that man can devise to hep God out of His little public relations slump. Too many of us have confused the church halls with the dance halls.

"Go into any city six weeks after a great 'City-Wide Revival' has been conducted. Look around the beer halls, the theaters, the people of the city and see if you can find evidence of a move of God. Generally speaking, there will be none.

"A true revival is a move of the Spirit of God. People become sponges soaked in the water of the Spirit. They just cannot help leaving a little of that water wherever they might walk. There are changes in the general population of that area as the Spirit of God moves through the people of God.

"Now, look at a church after their annual Spring Revival. Let's not dwell on that picture very long lest we hurt the feelings of the people in the pew. The pew is simply a place to sit and feel useful. It rarely finds use for the message and outreach for God.

"Why has all of this happened? It is because we have departed from the Words of the message which God has inspired and preserved for His people. Our 'best efforts' are just not 'doing the job.' Isn't it time that we just let the Words of God be the Words of God and meditate upon them? And use them as He calls us to do!"

In Psalm 11, the third verse, David asks a very sobering question:

'If the foundations be destroyed, what can the righteous do?'

The answer appears to be that we can do little of substance when we forsake all trust in the precious Words of God's inspired and preserved Book.

CHAPTER 9

WE DEPARTED FROM THE BOOK, THE TRUE WORDS OF GOD

As Israel of old departed from seeking the One, True God of Creation, so have we departed from the Book founded upon the True Words of God. The Traditional Text has been called by many names. It has been called **the Traditional Text, the Received Text, the Byzantine Text and the Syrian Text.**

It could more accurately called, "the Universal Text." It is not a localized text such as the Alexandrian which has been found most often in the sands of Gnostic Egypt. The Traditional Text has been found in all areas where the true churches flourished. It is upon this text of history which the King James Bible is based.

We are often reminded that there have been many discoveries of ancient texts in the past 400+ years since the first publication of the King James Bible. There are two things of which we are rarely informed in relation to these texts.

First, most of these discoveries are in affinity with the Traditional Text.

Second, the vast majority of those which disagree with the Traditional Text come from the dry and arid sand of Egypt. While this was a place where old manuscripts were more likely to survive the years, these were often manuscripts made from a pervasive Gnostic influence.

There is a **third** thing: Almost all of the preferred readings considered by the Critical Text people were available and rejected by the translating committee of the Authorized Bible of 1611. These were obviously available as they were contained in the Catholic English Bible of 1581.

We must admit that the true text of inspired and preserved Scripture has been, in several locations and times, sullied by false religionists. We see this in the *house text* of such as the Jehovah's

Witness cult. We see this in the Gnostic text of the Alexandrian text preferred by the modern-day critics. We can also see this in other false texts such as the Latin Vulgate of Jerome which the Roman Church pronounced as the true text even as they raised this text above any Greek texts.

It was a great boon to the European Churches when the Muslim hordes overran the Byzantine Empire. The Greek Speaking people of the Byzantine Empire carried the True Greek text of the original New Testament with them when they fled.

God raised up Erasmus to cull the chaff from the wheat as he spent years studying the Greek Text of Scripture and restoring its integrity with his labors and what would come to be called the Textus Receptus.

We must also consider that, much as the Jehovah's Witness' produced a "Bible" attuned to their distinctive doctrinal stands; so also did the Roman Church with Jerome's Vulgate and the Gnostic texts from Egypt.

History records no Holy Ghost revival by the use of these texts. History does record the history of the Protestant Reformation with the coming of the True Text base back into the enclaves of Europe. History also records the names of men like Moody, Billy Sunday, John R. Rice, and many more who saw great results for God as they preached from The Bible based on the Traditional Text.

I would like to consider Matthew 28:29 and Luke 22:31-32 with special emphasis on the English Language used in the 1611Authorized Version.

In Matthew 28:20 we read:

> *"Teaching them to observe all things whatsoever I have commanded you: and, lo, I am with you alway, even unto the end of the world. Amen."*

Do we see a *misprint* in this verse? Should the word be "always" rather than "alway?" The use of the early English language is often maligned by readers of the KJB. But the early English was, in many ways, actually a fuller language than that we have today.

The word "always" speaks of going from point A in time to point B. "Alway," however, has a deeper meaning. Jesus was saying that He would be with them – and that He would be available to them at each point of their journey. In a sense, Jesus was not saying that He would be at the terminus as the train of time rolled into a new station. He was saying that He would be available to His disciples on the train for the entire journey.

I'd also like to consider Luke 22:31-32 in the King James Bible, and see that it carries a deeper meaning than the modern versions will admit:

> "*21 And the Lord said, Simon, Simon, behold Satan hath desired to have you, that he may sift you as wheat: 22 But I have prayed for thee, that thy faith fail not: and when thou are converted, strengthen thy brethren.*"

Here we see those often-derided words, "Thee and thou." But they are superior as they give a fuller understanding of the text. It is helpful to understand that the "Y" words (You, Your, Ye) speak to a group of people rather than to a single individual. The "T" words (Thee, Thou, Thine) speak to a single person.

Did you get it? In the above verse from Luke, Jesus is warning Peter that Satan was going to assault all the disciples. Then the Lord says, "Peter, I am praying for you." Now, I would obviously believe that Jesus prayed for all of the disciples. But this was a tender moment for Peter to recall after he had so denied his Lord at the arrest and trial.

How wonderfully gracious is our Lord! There was no "question mark" needed after that affirmation of our Lord's care and love for us!

We often forget that Peter, as well as Judas, betrayed Jesus that night. It wasn't the same denial, of course. Judas betrayed Jesus into the hands of those who sought to kill Him. Peter only betrayed that He was a follower of Jesus.

Here is a little *back-story* about Peter.

> " *31 And he* [Jesus] *began to teach them, that the Son of man must suffer many things, and be rejected of the elders, and of the chief priests, and scribes, and be killed, and after three days rise again. *32* And he spake that saying openly. And Peter took him, and began to rebuke him. *33* But when he had turned about and looked on his disciples, he rebuked Peter, saying, Get thee behind me Satan: for thou savourest not the things that be of God, but the things that be of men.*"
> (Mark 8:31-33)

Jesus openly began to teach about His coming death. Peter said, not on my watch will you die! Jesus realized that this attitude was a carnal attitude and rebuked Peter. But the thought had been planted in Peter's mind that he needed to protect Jesus.

After cutting the ear off one of those guards brought to the Garden by Judas, and seeing Jesus heal the servant so attacked, Peter was ready for his *John Wayne* moment. He followed the procession to the place where Jesus was roughly interrogated. But, when he got there, and saw all the other men with swords, Peter had an epiphany. "Don't know Him." "I never saw Him." "Jesus, Who?"

I would believe that this was all within the hearing of Jesus. Look at Luke 22:60-62:

> " *60 And Peter said, Man, I know not what thou sayest. And immediately, while he yet spake, the cock crew. *61* And the Lord turned, and looked upon Peter. And Peter remembered the word of the Lord, how he had said unto him, Before the cock crow, thou shalt deny me thrice. *62* And Peter went out, and wept bitterly.*"

114

I believe that when Jesus looked upon Peter, it was with eyes of love and understanding. That is the way of our Lord. He understands the pain of the repentant heart. When we do repent of our sins, we receive a heart full of joy to replace the pain and sorrow of sin. A restored relationship with the Lord is a great joy in our spirit.

Well, I've spent several pages giving arguments as to why I accept not only an inspired Bible, but also a preserved Bible. What did Jesus have to say on this subject?

Luke 16:17:

> *"And it is easier for heaven and earth to pass, than one tittle of the law to fail."*

And, Matthew 5:18:

> *"For verily I say unto you, Till heaven and earth pass, one jot or one tittle shall in no wise pass from the law, till all be fulfilled."*

One more, from Matthew 24:35:

> *"Heaven and earth shall pass away: but my words shall not pass away."*

It seems abundantly clear that Jesus did not believe that the Words of Scripture would pass away and need to be replaced by theologians who only accept the general concept of the *"God Story."*

"OLDEST AND BEST" MANUSCRIPTS

About those two "oldest and best" manuscripts cited in the margins of even our King James Bible. These are the Codex Sinaiticus and the Vaticanus manuscript. We must note that the Vaticanus was found in the library of the Roman Catholic Church. This, we may recall is the very organization that departed from the Greek text and adopted the Latin of Jerome as the standard Scriptural text many centuries ago.

A FORGERY

As for the Codex Sinaiticus, it seems that this was a forgery from the early years of the nineteenth century. Get the book, "Forging of the Codex Sinaiticus, The; Cooper, Bill; Christian Science Movement; Portsmouth, UK; 2016." Look up the information at **www.csm.org.uk**. I understand that the book is also available in an "e-book" format from Amazon. When you have the book, look at the picture on page 72. An actual page from the Sinaiticus is shown. This page has an interesting cut. From the left margin, as might follow the red line on a three-hole piece of paper from a college binder. The cut then turns to the right and cuts off the paper just below where the writing must have been.

The book listed above will also provide the purpose of Simonides' in fabricating a forgery.

This is not the work of fire, age or worms. This is an obvious destruction made for a purpose. This purpose seems to be to remove any marks made by Constantine Simonides, the confessed forger of the *codex*. He claimed to have made certain marks on certain pages, to prove that he was indeed the fabricator of the forgery. Get the book and read his entire recounting of the event.

We have looked at some of the national sins which we've "enjoyed" in recent years. We have tried to explain what might be wrong. What are the ways in which we can return to being "normal" Christians even in this age of sin and lack of spiritual power?

A few years ago, a book came out by Francis A. Schaeffer. The question was asked, "How then should we live?" Let us look at just a few verses from the inspired and preserved volume of God's instructions.

We have actually stated the obvious early in this paper. We should work to grow the strength of the church. It has been said that the Christian church has always been one generation from extinction. There is a current cultural plea to *"pay it forward"* concerning the charity which is shown to us. Likewise, we need to *"pray it forward"* with the gospel message of the good news of salvation. Once we have realized our own salvation at the cross, it is to be expected that we would offer this same soul liberating experience to others. We are expected to evangelize the world around us.

"STEEL OURSELVES"

I have touched upon that rather extensively at the beginning of this paper. But we also need to "steel ourselves" in order to engage in this sort of spiritual warfare.

I think that a good place to begin our examination of walking as Christians in our daily lives begins with a reasonable walk. Walk into the doors of a local assembly of like-minded Biblical Christians. We are given this instruction in Hebrews 10:25:

> *"Not forsaking the assembling of ourselves together, as the manner of some is; but exhorting one another: and so much the more, as ye see the day approaching."*

THE DAY OF THE LORD'S APPEARING

The day of the Lord's appearing is approaching. As we look around us, we must be amazed about how the "signs of the times" bear more and more the shadows of the approach of the Lord to call His church out of this world and into the safety of Heaven. The *man of sin – the antichrist* will then step on the throne of the world. Seven real years of severe tribulation will be ushered upon the world. We can best prepare our friends and neighbors for this time of trial, even after we are removed from this world by helping them to prepare by coming to the Lord.

Our attendance with a group of friends at a Biblical church assembly will give us added training in the Scripture. This training will help us to further understand the spiritual issues which daily confront us. The fellowship of the other Christians, who should be among our closest friends in this earth, will give us courage – even as our own presence adds courage to those friends, to walk closer to the Lord with each passing day.

We really cannot function fully as Christians without a solid base of that weekly fellowship with other believers at a Christ-centered, Biblical-centered church. To paraphrase from the *"Halley's Bible Handbook:"* We should never see our attendance at a worship service on the Lord's Day as a mere habit. But we do need to be habitual in our attendance.

Do we really believe that we have the right to call ourselves followers of Christ as we neglect the only social institution which He founded for those who follow Him?

As we consider the need to live as Christians in the world, it would be good to consider the Words of Jesus from "The Great Commission" as given in Matthew 28:18-20:

> *[18] And Jesus came and spake unto them, saying, All power is given unto me in heaven and in earth. [19] Go ye therefore, and teach all nations, baptizing them in the name of the Father, and of the Son, and of the Holy Ghost: [20] Teaching them to observe all things whatsoever I have commanded you: and, lo, I am with you alway, even unto the end of the world. Amen."*

Verse 18. Jesus came to speak to His disciples. This is just another proof of the veracity of His resurrection. This was not a "long view" of someone who might have looked like Jesus from a distance. There could have been no mistake that this was, indeed, the Risen Savior. The way He looked was the One they had known for several years. The way He talked, even His mannerisms, were well known to His disciples. It was Him; there was no possibility of not recognizing the risen Savior. The joy that must have flooded their souls at this intimate instance.

Even the voice of the Savior was known. He spoke to them. they would have listened very closely to this man they had witnessed murdered just a few short days before. Now He was there and there was no doubt about that it was He Who was speaking to them. How often they had listened to His teaching. How much more would they listen to a Savior Who was risen from the dead.

Just consider how you would react and listen to if you were to find that father or mother, brother or friend, who you had saw in a casket and at the internment at a cemetery, as they began to speak. This was more than simply "someone," this was the man who had the words of life. (John 6:68)

JESUS' POWER

Jesus claimed total authority. I spent several years in the military. In point of fact, I am now receiving a military pension. When one who is in a position of authority speaks, we must listen. Note that this is not because we might like or respect that person. If nothing else, we listen because that person speaks from a position of authority. Jesus claimed, and exhibited total authority not in a group, not even by an appearance of authority. When One speaks after having raised from the dead, it would behoove us to give an ear to his words. Jesus is Lord. We call Him such. We have a total spiritual need to treat Him as such. His slightest wish is our command. He here gives us commands as how we should work and live at His followers!

Verse 19. I remember men from the "World War II" generation telling me receiving their draft notices. They told me that their draft notices began with the words "Your friends and neighbors from the local draft board…" My Vietnam Era draft notice was more to the point, "You are hereby ordered to report to such and such a place for induction into the United States Armed Forces."

In verse 18 Jesus had said that He had all power. That word power is number 1849 in Strong's. It is defined as "(in the sense of ability); privilege, i.e. (subjectively) force, capacity, competency, freedom, or (objectively) mastery (concretely, magistrate, superhuman, potentate, token of control), delegated influence:--authority, jurisdiction, liberty, power, right, strength."

I think that we do this word no violence by understanding it as "authority." There was a saying in Basic Training – "If the drill sergeant tells you to jump, ask him 'how high' on the way up." Jesus has more authority than that for us.

Essentially, Jesus said, "I have the authority to demand this of you, therefore... Do we really wish to be telling Him, "No, I don't think so." Try that answer in a human military. Jesus has more right than a military commander to call us. We are saved because of His sacrifice on the Cross of Calvary.

There is more authority than just His right to call us to follow Him. He offers to us the power of His authority as we do spiritual battle with the forces of darkness.

It is those "forces of darkness" that we encounter as we teach others of the ways of the pure religion of Jesus. That is part of our task. Again, this is just one reason that we are to unite with a local body of believers so that we might both be strengthened by them and in turn strengthen them by our presence. As we do this, we will learn more of the Savior and of our duties and privileges under Him.

BAPTISM

Verse 19 and 20. Not only are we to teach, we are to baptize. I found an old copy of my original baptismal certificate. I actually remember the experience. I only got my hair wet. Later I was baptized according to the Biblical meaning of the world. The word baptize is not a translated word. It is based on the Greek Word (number 907 in Strong's. "baptizo, to immerse, submerge; to make whelmed (i.e. fully wet); used only (in the New Testament) of ceremonial ablution, especially (technically) of the ordinance of Christian baptism:--Baptist, baptize, wash." Sadly, it is transliterated in King James Bibles. And, in almost all the *fake* bibles translated from the Critical Text. That is as close to a complaint as I can make of the KJB.

Please note that there is no "saving grace" even in Biblical

120

baptism. It comes after the teaching of salvation has been accepted by a person. Only a person already saved from his sin is a true candidate for baptism.

In ancient times this was associated with the joining of a fellowship of believers. Only those already born-again are candidates to join a local assembly. An unbeliever is not a fit candidate to join a church.

ONE GOD

Consider that the believer is baptized in THE Name of the Father, THE Name of the Son and THE Holy Spirit. The Father, Son, and Holy Spirit is One God. There are not three god's worshipped in the Christian Religion. There is only One God eternally existent in three distinct Persons. I cannot adequately explain this concept but, since the Bible teaches this concept, I do accept it fully and without hesitation.

I have written a large book, *"The Deity of Jesus, the Christ."* Trying to explain this truth. It is available at **http://theoldpathspublications.com/Pages/BookStore.htm**. If you don't "do" computers, just write to me: E. E. DeWitt, P.O. Box 4, Woodhull, IL 61490 and I'll get the information out to you.

Verse 20. Note that the concept of teaching does not end. We are taught to go out into the world and teach others. Then we return to the study of the Scripture and the discipline of the local assembly and continue to be taught the things of God.

GO

In both verse 19 and 20 we are told to "go." Christianity is not a static religion. We are to constantly struggle to learn more of the Savior and try to further model our own lives to be more like His blessed Presence.

I have noticed that our speech tends to take on the tenor of those with whom we associate. I spoke one way in high school. I began to speak differently when I went to college. I spoke another way while I was in the military. I did not become more profane in my speech in the military but it was different that when it had been in college.

That is another reason that we should unite with like-minded believers in a local assembly. We will tend to become more like those with whom we associate. May we also associate with our Lord more often, through the reading of Scripture and prayer. In this our personalities may take on more of the manner of the Savior. This will help our own spiritual life and make us more likely to reach out to call others to salvation.

Calling others to salvation is the "Order of the Day" for Christians. "The Order of the Day" is a foundational part of military life. It is part of the daily life of the soldier. It is what the soldier is to do every day.

I spent much of the first part of this paper explaining that need for evangelizing the world about us. That Christian witness needs to be an integral part of our daily life in this life. "Hi; how are you?" "Pretty Good. I am saved and on my way to Heaven. How about you?"

ABOUT THE AUTHOR

In the past 50 years, Dr. DeWitt has pastored four churches in Louisiana and Illinois. He is currently retired from the active pastorate; he was born in north central Illinois. He was a combat infantryman during the Vietnamese Conflict and won his Combat Infantry Badge less than three weeks after entering the war zone.

Dr. DeWitt has written books on Inspiration, the transmission of the traditional text, the Virgin Birth of Jesus, among others. He has also written verse by verse commentaries on the Catholic (non-Pauline) epistles of the New Testament, and Daniel. Also, he is currently near completion of a book to include the Minor Prophets of the Old Testament.

Dr. DeWitt taught the fundamentals of the Christian Religion over WGPA-TV 7 in Galesburg, Illinois from 1985 – 1995. He also published a newsletter, "BQM Reports." This started out to be simply a newsletter of his activities. It soon morphed into a bi-monthly journal of theological thought and teaching. The magazine had a press run of about @1000 every two months; at least one copy was sent to every state in the U.S. and all the provinces of Canada. Copies were sent to every continent except Antarctica.

Dr. DeWitt has been a member of MENSA and Intertel, which require evidence of a high IQ. He is a graduate both from private and public colleges and universities.

Dr. DeWitt was married to the former Linda Guenther for over thirty years until her Home Going to Glory in May of 2000. They are the parents of two children, Amy and Ethan, and have two grandchildren, Shandi and Elijah.

www.ingramcontent.com/pod-product-compliance
Lightning Source LLC
Chambersburg PA
CBHW071137090426
42736CB00012B/2146